B+T ~3/66

Mass
Persuasion
in
Communist
China

Mass Persuasion in Communist China

by

Tê-chi Yü

FREDERICK T. C. YU

FREDERICK A. PRAEGER, *Publisher*
New York • London

FREDERICK A. PRAEGER, PUBLISHER
64 UNIVERSITY PLACE, NEW YORK 3, N.Y., U.S.A.
77-79 CHARLOTTE STREET, LONDON W. 1, ENGLAND

Published in the United States of America in 1964 by
Frederick A. Praeger, Inc., *Publisher*

Printed in the United States of America

To
Siao-fen, my wife

PREFACE

This is an attempt to understand how mass persuasion is conceived, developed, and manipulated by the Chinese Communists as an instrument of power and a method of control. It is an exploratory study—nothing more. I have based my study almost exclusively on Chinese Communist publications. The difficulties involved in using such data are too well known to scholars on Communist affairs to need any discussion here. It should suffice to note that throughout I have tried only to describe and analyze mass persuasion as it is presented in these sources: I report and interpret; I do not praise or condemn.

The book is the result of intermittent research that began in 1951 when I joined the research staff of the Department of Asiatic Studies of the University of Southern California. During my two-year association with the Chinese Documents Project, which was directed by Professor Theodore H. E. Chen, I completed several reports on Chinese Communist propaganda. Two such reports were published as monographs by the Human Resources Research Institute. I did not have a chance to follow up on these studies until 1958–59, when I was Ford Foundation postdoctoral fellow at the Center for International Studies at the Massachusetts Institute of Technology and the Department of Social Relations at Harvard University. A rough draft of this present book manuscript was ready in 1959 when I left Cambridge to return to my teaching post at the School of Journalism at Montana State University. Unhappily, a conspiracy of events prevented me from doing much further work on the manuscript until 1961 after my return from a trip to Asia.

It is impossible to acknowledge adequately the many people who have helped me in the preparation of this book, either knowingly or unknowingly. I extend my thanks to all of them, even if I can single out only a few of them for special mention here.

I owe a great intellectual debt to Professor Theodore H. E. Chen of the University of Southern California, who first encouraged me to undertake this study. I also owe an embarrassingly large debt to Mr. Harold R. Isaacs of the MIT Center for International Studies. Without his friendly interest and sustained encouragement, this book would not have been completed.

I am grateful to Professors Daniel Lerner, Ithiel de Sola Pool, and Lucien Pye—all of the Massachusetts Institute of Technology; and to Professor Gordon W. Allport and the late Professor Samuel Stouffer, both of Harvard University, for inspiration and advice.

I express my thanks to Dean Edward W. Barrett of the Columbia University Graduate School of Journalism, whose kind support was an important factor bringing this book to publication.

I am deeply indebted to Miss Hanna Gunther and Mrs. Elizabeth Sifton of Frederick A. Praeger, Inc., for their pointed criticisms, useful suggestions and patient assistance. It was a genuine pleasure to work with such charming and able editors.

Grateful acknowledgments are due to the Ford Foundation for a postdoctoral fellowship that enabled me to spend an unusually happy and profitable year at Cambridge; to the MIT Center for International Studies; and to its director, Dr. Max F. Millikan, for all the support and assistance that made possible a large part of the actual writing for this volume.

I owe a special debt of thanks to Miss Barbara Cohen, my research assistant. She did some heroic typing, read the proof, and prepared the index. She approached such taxing chores with unfailing intelligence and enthusiasm, and she gave me many discerning editorial suggestions.

And finally, my gratitude to my wife, who had far more to do with this book than she realizes.

Needless to add, nobody but myself is responsible for errors or shortcomings in the book.

Frederick T. C. Yu

New York City
December, 1963

CONTENTS

Mass
Persuasion
in
Communist
China

1. THE ROLE AND NATURE OF MASS PERSUASION: SOCIALIZATION OF THE MINDS

One of the most striking characteristics of the Chinese Communist Party is its shrewd manipulation of coercive and persuasive communications as an instrument of power and a method of control. In spite of their dictatorial qualities, the rulers in Peking do not govern the nation solely by naked force. They have always depended upon mass hypnotic indoctrination and stirring persuasion to facilitate the tasks of the Party leadership and to mobilize the minds and effort of the population.

That persuasive communications always play a vital role in a Communist state is hardly surprising. For in a Communist or totalitarian state, solidarity and advancement, it is generally believed, depend upon ideological unanimity, and communications transmit the model with which it is expected that everyone will conform. In fact, every government in history, one can be sure, resorts to some kind of persuasion for one purpose or another.

But mass persuasion in Communist China is a startlingly new phenomenon, new both to China and to world Communism. Although the idea of controlling the thoughts and actions of the populace is not totally strange in China, no precedent can be found in Chinese history for mass ideological conversion of the sort now attempted by the Communists. Although many of the techniques of persuasion used by the Peking regime are obviously borrowed from or inspired by those found in the Soviet Union, the Bolshevik effort to remold the thinking of the Russian population (not just Party members and government cadres) in the post-

3

1917 era can hardly be compared with the Chinese Marxists' attempt, in intensity, scope, or skill.

Indeed, this phenomenon is new in the entire history of communication. It is new in that the Chinese Communist system of persuasive and coercive communications encompasses almost all feasible vehicles of human expression and means of influencing attitude and behavior. It is a communication system that brings the largest possible number of Chinese people into direct and close contact with the Party. It is designed not only to produce among the masses the particular thoughts and attitudes desired by the Party, but also to provide the Party with a continuous flow of information concerning the sentiments of the people. It is a communication system that is conscientiously administered and vigorously utilized by the Party so as to assure itself that what ought to be known by the people *is* known and that what should be felt by the people *is* felt.

A master key to understanding the extremely important role of mass persuasion in Communist China is the Chinese Marxists' dictum that "thought determines action." It is with utmost seriousness that they insist that "politics should take command" in everything done in the country. The following editorial of the official paper *Jen Min Jih Pao* (*People's Daily*) is typical of this reasoning:

> Work is done by man, and man's action is governed by his thinking. A man without the correct political thinking is a man without a soul. If politics does not take command—i.e., if the proletarian ideology does not take command—there can be no direction. In every work we undertake, we must always insist that politics take command and let political and ideological work come before anything else. Only when we are both thorough and penetrating with our political and ideological work can we guarantee the accomplishment of our task.[2]

In other words, if people can be made to think "correctly," according to the Communists, they will naturally act "correctly." The Chinese Communists seem to be quite determined to make this point, and their press is flooded with stories of how various tasks are accomplished under almost impossible conditions mainly because, to use a Communist expression, "the correct political and ideological work takes command." It may be the task of killing 1.7 million catties of flies in one day in Peking[3]; it may be the task of making Chinese intellectuals *chiao hsin* or "give their heart" to the Party.[4] How much truth there is in such stories is not the point; what is significant is the Communists' nearly fanatic faith in their "correct political and ideological work." Consider, for instance, such popular newspaper headlines as: "Once the Problem of Ideology is Solved, the Problem of Food is Solved"[5]; "Politics Takes Command: Production of Iron and Steel Goes Up"[6]; "Ideological and Political Work is the Lifeline of Economic Work."[7]

One is understandably inclined to dismiss all this as idle propaganda talk, typical Marxist gobbledygook, or characteristic hypocritical attempts to maintain a false front of democracy. But such Communist verbiage is not entirely meaningless. It is at least suggestive of the Communist superstition about the miraculous power of political or ideological indoctrination; it certainly indicates the presence of intensive propaganda or tireless persuasion in virtually every task undertaken by the Party.

It almost seems that the Chinese Communists have gone somewhat beyond the Marxist dogma which maintains that changes in a society are determined by its political and economic systems. They seem to believe that attitudes, opinions, ideas, and thoughts must first be revolutionized, in order to build a solid foundation for the planned political, economic, social, and cultural changes. Mao Tse-tung most certainly had this in mind when he declared, shortly after his conquest of the Chinese mainland, that the method of persuasion was to be used among the people "on a nation-wide and over-all scale." His aim, as he expressed it earlier in his oft-quoted book *On People's Democratic Dictatorship*, was:

> To educate and re-educate themselves, to free themselves from the influence of reactionaries at home and abroad . . . to unlearn the bad habits and thoughts acquired from the old society and not let themselves travel on the erroneous path pointed out by the reactionaries, but to continue to develop toward socialist and Communist society.[8]

Clearly, the Chinese Communists are not content with producing merely obedient, docile subjects. They have a new gospel to preach, a new society to build, and a new world to construct.

They want converts and believers, not just skeptical or opportunistic followers. They require enthusiastic support of the people, not just silent acceptance. They possess what they consider *the* truth; they cannot tolerate "heresies." They want to capture and remold the minds of the entire population.

This is a big order. For it means no less than an all-out ideological assault on one-fifth of the human race. Nevertheless, it is exactly the goal the Chinese Communists have vowed to achieve. This is precisely the task they have set out to do with their penetrating system of persuasive and coercive communications—a task upon which they have spent more time, effort, and energy than they have upon any other activity in the country.

Strictly speaking, mass persuasion in Communist China is the process of socialization of the minds of the people. For, to the Chinese Marxists, the creation of the "new Socialist man" is a prerequisite of the building of the "new Socialist state." This is the one singularly important process of socialization upon which all others depend.

It is, therefore, no wonder that in the lexicon of the Chinese Communists, propaganda (*hsien chuan*) and persuasion (*shuo fu*) are always described as "ideological warfare" or "political warfare," to be "vigorously fought on every conceivable front at all times." This is regarded as the "fundamental form of class struggle" and utilized as "the basic working method of the Chinese Communist Party."[9] This is considered a "sentinel battle" in all political and economic struggles.[10]

Indeed, few statements are made by the Chinese Communists with more seriousness and higher frequency than their loud cry for penetrating and thorough propaganda and persuasion. At the Second Session of the Eighth National Congress of their Party, in 1958, for instance, they declared once again:

> Ideological and political work is always the soul and guide of every kind of work. In every case, abandonment or neglect of ideological and political work by the Party will divorce us from the masses and lead us astray.[11]

A professional Communist propagandist expresses this even more explicitly:

To pay attention only to the job to be done and not to pay attention to the raising of the political and ideological consciousness of the masses to a higher level will not result in good work. The job might be considered done in terms of form and statistics, but politically and ideologically it is still undone.

There is a long-range objective in whatever work we are doing, and that is to march through New Democracy to socialism. Therefore, in whatever work we undertake, we must pay great attention to the task of carrying on the education of the people in Marxism-Leninism, so that they can help build up the New Democracy of today and walk into the socialism in the future. We must make every Chinese citizen, after going through this propaganda education, visualize the bright picture of the future and therefore struggle aggressively for its realization. Otherwise, our work will be deadly colorless, lacking in political content, routine, and eventually mistaken.[12]

The Study of Mass Persuasion

It should be readily apparent that what is meant by mass persuasion in this study bears little resemblance to what is regarded as mass persuasion in the field of communications and opinion study. For instance, Merton's well-known work on mass persuasion is a study of a campaign[13]; Lippmann[14] and Mills[15] are interested in communication and persuasion as social, rather than political, phenomena. Hovland, Janis and Kelley, in their experimental study of persuasive communication, mainly stress such matters as motivation, personality factors, and the influence of social roles on resistance to acceptance of new ideas.[16]

Indeed, there is an impressive amount of literature on problems of communication and persuasion. While most studies do suggest some principles that may operate under various political situations, they deal with a social context that is too un-Chinese to be of much conceptual value here.

Reference must be made to a considerable body of literature on one special aspect of persuasion in Communist China: the problem of brainwashing. Much of what is reported and analyzed in the studies on this subject offers helpful insight into the understanding of Communist indoctrination. But most of them deal only with the Chinese handling of prisoners of war, treatment of the "enemies of the state," and indoctrination of Chinese intellectuals.[17]

Inkeles' brilliant and penetrating study of public opinion in Soviet Russia comes closest to what is attempted here. His work, an illustrious investigation of the mass media in the Soviet Union, is a great contribution to the understanding of the concept of propaganda and agitation in a Communist state.

The nature of mass persuasion in Communist China, however, requires that the scope of exploration in a study of it be much larger than that for an investigation of the mass media per se. For it is also necessary to examine the attempt at mass ideological conversion that seems to be the distinctive feature of Chinese Communist efforts.[18] And this rather uncommon phenomenon of mass persuasion raises a host of questions for students of communication and opinion.

First, there are questions about its general scheme: What is the master plan of mass persuasion? How is it conceived? How is it related to the general plan of the Communist revolution? What are the guiding principles of persuasion policy? What are the strategies, tactics, and techniques? What and how many of the techniques are modifications of Soviet or other totalitarian models, and how many of them, if any, are creations of the Chinese Communists? What is the design of the persuasion apparatus? How is it controlled and how does it operate? Where and how does coercion enter into the picture?

Second, there are questions about the media and contents of persuasion: What is the developmental pattern of persuasive communications? What are the channels and means of communication? What are the characteristics of each? Why and how does each arrive at its particular characteristics? What are the major contents of persuasion?

Third, there are questions about the effects of persuasion: How does the Chinese population react to mass persuasion? What are the changes of beliefs and attitudes? What actually goes on in the minds of those who are indoctrinated? Who, how many, and how are the people won over by the persuasive communications? Are there people who have built walls around their minds? What has happened to those who resisted persuasion? What are the cultural and societal changes that have resulted from the mass persuasion?

There are, of course, other questions. But these should suffice to illustrate the breadth and complexity of this peculiar system of mass communication and social control and to suggest the problems this study seeks to elucidate.

This study does not pretend to answer all the questions. It has only two objectives in mind: (1) to examine and interpret the Chinese Communist attempt at mass ideological conversion, or remolding of the population, and (2) to describe and analyze how the system of persuasive communications works in Communist China. It is hoped that achievement of the two tasks will result in a reasonably clear and comprehensive picture.

Ideally, of course, a study of this kind should include data from on-the-spot observation or direct interview with the people in China. At the moment, this is clearly out of the question for students in the West. But direct contact with the Chinese people does not necessarily guarantee satisfactory answers. This is illustrated rather vividly by the former French Premier, Edgar Faure, who visited Red China in 1956 and who was so puzzled by the then much-publicized "Hundred Flowers" campaign and other movements that he wrote: "One must be Chinese, and, without doubt, also a good Communist to understand them. At least, one must have been in China, as I was able to be . . . to understand what one does not understand."[19]

Perhaps it is true that many aspects of mass persuasion in Communist China are not always easy for a Western visitor to understand, partly because the phenomenon is virtually unique and partly because it is based on a logic that is not part of a Westerner's frame of reference. But this does not mean that it is so mysterious and complex as to defy comprehension. As a matter of fact, one can learn a great deal by examining what the Chinese Marxists have to say on the subject and by analyzing the contents of the Communist persuasive communications. While it is true that Communists are rarely communicative about their motives and actions, the Peking regime is not at all reticent about its work in propaganda, agitation, and indoctrination. Indeed, a considerable amount of information is available on the subject and it offers many clues to the purpose, operations, and problems of mass persuasion.

2. THEORY AND POLICY

It has been said that, "In the Soviet system, there is not a theory of state and a theory of communication; there is only one theory."[1] Essentially the same can be said of Communist China.

This does not mean, of course, that Communists rarely theorize about communications. It merely suggests that the Marxist-Leninist dogma that shapes the course of development in every Communist society necessarily determines every policy and activity of the Party. The best place, then, to start an investigation of the theory and policy of communication in a Communist country is the Communist ideology itself.

1. Class Consciousness

The Chinese Communist revolution is a process of class struggle, and the entire course of Chinese Communist propaganda and agitation stems from one fundamental concept—class consciousness. This concept permeates the whole structure of Communist state and society; the central purpose of propaganda, so a favorite Communist cliché goes, is to "awaken, heighten, and sharpen the class consciousness of the masses," from which the real strength and power of the Party are supposed to generate. Ai Ssu-ch'i, one of the best-known interpreters and writers of Marxism-Leninism-Stalinism-Maoism in China, puts it quite neatly:

> Politics . . . is nothing but a centralized form of class struggle.
> . . . The fundamental content of our Party's political task is to raise the level of consciousness of the revolutionary class, to pull together forces of all the revolutionary classes to oppose the control of the reactionary class and fight for the possession of the power to rule the nation. . . . There are only two kinds of political tasks:

11

one is the task of propaganda and education, and the other is the task of organization. Both aim at raising the level of political consciousness of the revolutionary class, uniting with the forces of the revolutionary classes and fighting for the ruling power.[2]

This is a logical place to ask the question raised by Glantz: "Is a class a class because 'thinking makes it so,' or is a class a class purely on objective grounds?"[3] Should one follow MacIver's notion that class consciousness is necessarily antecedent to the existence of classes[4] or Durkheim's idea that an individual can never recruit himself into a class by psychological invention?[5] To Glantz, "a class is not the product of its consciousness, but develops into a self-conscious class when its members become aware of their objective conditions."[6]

But these are general views of class consciousness. The Communist brand is something else, and it is important also to keep in mind the difference between the Marxist and Leninist approaches to the matter. For Marx, class consciousness is the basis of political consciousness. But Lenin goes further—and this is perhaps his greatest contribution to the propaganda of Marxism—arguing that class consciousness left to itself becomes entirely bound up in the "economic struggle" and will be confined to a mere "trade-unionist" consciousness, that therefore class consciousness must be awakened, educated, and brought into the battle in a larger sphere than the worker-employer relationship alone, and that this task should be assigned only to an elite group of professional revolutionaries, "the conscious vanguard of the proletariat."[7]

It is the Leninist interpretation of class consciousness that is followed and stressed by the Chinese Communists, who reason in this manner: (1) In the revolutionary class struggle, self-emancipation of the masses is the only possible way to success; (2) self-emancipation is possible only when the masses reach the right level of political or class consciousness; (3) class consciousness cannot elevate itself to a higher level; it must be constantly and correctly stimulated so that it will neither go astray nor lead to a petty-bourgeois trade-unionist mentality; (4) only the Communist Party is qualified and able to lead the masses in the development of their consciousness because only the Communists have achieved the highest level of consciousness and the "correct" class viewpoint of the proletariat.

This interpretation of class consciousness is of great importance because it forms the ideological basis of Communist persuasion policy. Liu Shao-chi makes this unmistakably clear:

> With us, therefore, everything is dependent on and determined by the people's consciousness and self-activity, without which we can accomplish nothing and all our efforts will be in vain. But as long as we rely upon the consciousness and self-activity of the masses and as long as such consciousness and self-activity are genuine, then with the addition of the Party's correct leadership, every aspect of the great cause of the Party will finally triumph. Therefore, when the masses are not fully conscious, the duties of Communists—the vanguard of the masses of the people—in carrying out any kind of work is to develop their consciousness by every effective and suitable means. This is the first step in our work which must be done no matter how difficult it is or how much time it will take.
>
> Only when the first step has been taken can we enter upon the next step. In other words, when the masses have reached the necessary level of consciousness, it is then our responsibility to guide them in their action—to guide them to organize and fight. When this is brought about, we may further develop their consciousness through their actions. This is how we lead the masses step by step to fight for the basic slogans of the people as put forth by our Party.[8]

Take, for instance, the role of class consciousness in the propaganda of land reform, undoubtedly one of Red China's most celebrated programs. Emphasizing the importance of persuasion or "ideological struggle" in this form of class struggle, Ai Ssu-ch'i writes:

> Class struggle cannot be developed without ideological struggle. . . . The reason that the masses of peasants can stand up and take part in their struggle for land reform is mainly because they are awakened, enlightened and guided by the working class (the Communist Party) and possess the right consciousness. They no longer believe that landlords are born to be superior and have the right to oppress the peasants. . . . They now understand that it is not the peasants who depend upon landlords for a living but actually the landlords who depend upon the peasants. Therefore, only the con-

scious peasants who can ideologically degrade and look down on the landlord class have the courage for the struggle.[9]

Indeed, the entire land reform program is not just an important economic policy, as is often assumed, but a plan to enable the Chinese peasants to establish the "correct" class viewpoint and to engage in class struggle. One high-ranking Communist leader goes as far as to say: "The whole process of land reform is one of mobilizing the masses. It is a process through which the broad masses of peasants engage in struggle (*tou cheng*) against the landlord class and through which the peasants ceaselessly elevate their class consciousness to a higher level."[10] This is why Liu Shao-chi also says that "the ultimate objective of land reform is not purely the relief of poor peasants," but the "elimination of the landlord class" and the "abolition of the feudalistic land system."[11]

An official statement of the Party's propaganda authorities made this point crystal-clear:

> We request all government agencies responsible for land reform and all members of land reform work teams fully to understand: we reduce rent not simply for the sake of reducing rent, and we divide land not merely for the sake of dividing land. *Our fundamental objective is to make use of this [land reform] movement [and forthcoming movements] to raise the peasants' ideological and political consciousness to the level of opposing feudalism and imperialism and thus to form a powerful class army to struggle for this political objective. In order to achieve this objective we have to give the peasants some actual benefits or profits, on the one hand, but, on the other hand and at the same time, we have to develop fully the ideological and political education among workers* [italics added].[12]

One can readily see why the Chinese Communists, once fondly but mistakenly referred to as "agrarian reformers," have vigorously opposed the idea of "peaceful land reform." They say that it is better not to divide land among poor peasants at all than to divide it by peaceful methods. For to have land reform without a "fierce struggle [*tou cheng*] against the landlord class" would deny the Communist Party a unique opportunity for mass persuasion and class education. The fact that everyone in China, not merely the peasants, had to participate in this movement in the first few years of the regime certainly testifies to the indoctrinational value of the campaign.

2. Mass Line

"The fundamental policy of the Party," *Jen Min Jih Pao* editorialized, "is the policy of mass line."[13]

Like class consciousness, this mass line has become something of a political myth of the Chinese Communist Party. It is a policy to which almost every Communist Party member refers in almost every speech or writing for almost every occasion. They talk forever about the "harmonious unity with the masses," "the viewpoint of the masses," "wisdom of the masses," "sanction of the masses," etc. Almost every program or policy of the Party is "demanded," "desired," and "initiated" by the masses. It is the "creative initiative" and "highly elevated political consciousness" of the masses that result in their "volunteering" to go to the Korean front, "demanding" the suppression of "reactionaries, counter-revolutionaries and rightists," "insisting" on various mass movements, or "petitioning" for the realization of the commune program. It even appears that the Party rarely does anything without the "sanction of the masses." Nothing in Communist China, one can be sure, is or can be divorced from this seemingly sacred doctrine of mass line.

We must remember that the Communists reject both "commandism" and "tailism" as methods of leading the masses. We must remember further that class consciousness cannot elevate itself automatically. Now, how does this mass line operate? And how is it related to class consciousness and mass persuasion?

The answer can be found in the Communist formula that "the policy and methods of work of the Party must originate from the masses and go back to the masses." A cynical interpreter of this statement would argue that the Communists try to make the ideas of the Party sound as if they were ideas of the people. It is closer to the mark to say that they attempt to transform the feeling or sentiments of the masses into an idea or notion that, on the one hand, seemingly represents what the masses want, but on the other, expresses what the Party really intends.

As early as 1943, Mao wrote that he had no use for Communists who would "spend their whole life sitting indoors and never go out to weather the storm and see the world . . . the storm being the big storm of mass struggle, and the world being the big world of mass struggle."[14] Then Mao preached:

> We should go into the midst of the masses, learn from them, sum up their experiences so that these experiences will become well-defined principles and methods, and then explain them to the masses (through agitation work), and call upon the masses to put them into practice in order to solve their problems and lead them to liberation and happiness.[15]

This method of mass line was explained more fully by Mao on another occasion when he wrote:

> In all practical work of our Party, correct leadership can only be developed on the principle of "from the masses, to the masses." This means summing up (i.e. co-ordinating and systematizing after careful study) the views of the masses (i.e. views scattered and unsystematic), then taking the resulting ideas back to the masses, explaining and popularizing them until the masses embrace the ideas as their own, stand up for them and translate them into action by way of testing their correctness. Then it is necessary once more to sum up the views of the masses, and once again take the resulting ideas back to the masses so that the masses give them their wholehearted support. . . . And so on, over and over again, so that each time these ideas emerge with greater correctness and become more vital and meaningful. This is what the Marxist theory of knowledge teaches us.[16]

So much importance is attached by the Chinese Communists to this method of mass line that it is formalized as a general guide to action in the Party Constitution. Every Party member is urged to "ceaselessly develop the tradition of mass line in all tasks of the Party":

> Whether or not the Party leadership is correct depends upon the Party's ability to analyze, systematize, summarize and consolidate the opinions and experiences of the masses, to transform them as the policy of the Party and then to return them, through propaganda, agitation and organization, to the masses as their own guide to thinking and action.[17]

It must be remembered that the mass line is, as Liu Shao-chi takes great pains to point out, "class line, as mass line of the proletariat."[18] This means that while the Communists are constantly and keenly aware of the sentiments and desires of the masses, they do not necessarily accept any or every idea or opinion coming from them. The masses can have "wrong," even "backward," ideas when their "class consciousness is not adequately elevated." Moreover, the Communists add, the masses do not always see their way clearly because they are the targets of "evil propaganda" or "counterrevolutionary ideologies" of the bourgeois and capitalist classes. The *Jen Min Jih Pao* puts it rather bluntly: "Unquestionably, our mass line does not mean that we follow those believers of tailism who believe that we should do whatever the masses want. . . . Our slogan is: 'We do what must be done.' "[19]

In his analysis of the masses, Liu Shao-chi points out that there are generally three sections of the masses: "the relatively active elements, the intermediate elements and the backward elements"; and that the active elements are usually in the minority.[20] He adds:

> In accordance with the mass line, the majority, that is the intermediate and the backward elements, must be taken care of, otherwise the advanced sections will become isolated and nothing can be done satisfactorily. The slogans of action and the forms of struggle and of organization we put forward before the masses must be acceptable to the intermediate and the backward elements. The development of the self-consciousness and self-activity of the masses concerns chiefly these people. A mass movement is possible only when these people are awakened and inspired to action. . . .
>
> Our sole intention is to attract and to set in motion the intermediate and backward elements through the active elements. In other words, it is for rallying the broadest possible masses that the active elements are to be organized. If the intermediate and backward masses are not yet awakened, we must know how to enlighten them as well as how to wait for them.[21]

But how is this to be done? Liu, as one of the Party's leading theoreticians, has a good deal to say on the subject. He is especially shrewd in perceiving certain aspects of persuadability in this large mass of "intermediate and backward elements." He is convinced, for instance, that the class consciousness of these elements cannot be elevated merely through high-sounding theories or glittering slogans. Keenly aware that "the masses, especially the peasantry, usually consider problems on the basis of their personal experience instead of on the basis of our general propaganda and slogans," he prescribes the following approach:

> In our work we should break through at one point to give an example to the masses and let them see and understand things by themselves. Only by giving demonstrative examples to the masses can we encourage them, particularly the intermediate and backward elements, by affording them the opportunities and facilities to understand the problems, thereby instilling in them confidence and courage to act under our Party's slogans and to culminate in an upsurge of mass enthusiasm.
>
> The reason that recently army heroes, labour heroes and model workers in different places have been playing an outstanding role and have become the best propagandists and organizers of the masses is due to the very fact that through such living personalities, examples, and experiences familiar to the people the masses are enabled to understand the issues, thus heightening their consciousness and self-confidence. This also explains why revolutionary reconstruction in China's revolutionary bases is playing an educational and enlightening role for people of the whole nation and is developing the entire nation's consciousness and self-confidence.[22]

This emphasis on "personal experience of the masses," "demonstrative examples," and "living personalities" in the Party's attempt to "elevate the level of consciousness of the masses" has an important bearing on the policy and pattern of Communist mass persuasion. It helps to explain, for instance, why "aggressive elements" or "activists" must be constantly "discovered, cultivated, and utilized" to serve the persuasive function of every Communist campaign or movement, why a huge army of propagandists and agitators must be permanently maintained, why oral agitation must be integrated with written communication, why person-to-person communication must remain one of the major forms of propaganda, and why accusation meetings, *tou cheng* (struggle) meetings, or confession sessions are all considered effective means of communication.

3. The United Front

Like the concepts of class consciousness and mass line, what is known as the policy of united front is another political myth of the Chinese Communist Party. It is important because it suggests, though not always clearly, not only the direction of Communist propaganda but also some of the strategic and tactical principles of mass persuasion.

The Communist revolution, very clearly, is political warfare. Two processes are always involved in every kind of warfare: elimination of enemies and winning of friends. But the differentiation between friend and foe is not always a simple matter, at least not so far as the Communists are concerned. He who is accepted as a "friend" today may so "misunderstand" the Party or be "so hopelessly poisoned by incorrect ideologies" as to become an "enemy" of the proletariat tomorrow. An entire class that is branded "exploiting," "oppressive," and "obstructive" today may later be treated as an ally or as "thoroughly re-educated" and "constructively useful" to the cause of socialism. There are numerous cases of this in the history of every Communist Party in the world. The shifting of friends and foes and the choice of targets form the basis of Communist propaganda strategy.

The guiding principle of Communist political warfare is tersely summarized as follows: "to unite with all the people which can be united around us, to win over the neutrals so that they will not help the enemies, to make use of the conflicts among enemies and thus to disintegrate the enemy camp."[23]

Hardly anything original is suggested in this principle. But a certain Communist shrewdness is easily noticeable in the design and operation of the united front.

Mao, who has written a great deal on this subject, constantly refers to the united front as the "most fundamental strategic responsibility" or "basic political platform" of the Chinese Communist Party. While much of his thinking on the united front has direct relevance to the Party's propaganda policy, space will permit only a brief discussion here.

Throughout the history of the Chinese Communist Party, when the Communists were consolidating and expanding their political influence through their policy of the united front, tirelessly urging the "cooperation" and "concession" of other groups or classes, they never for one moment lost sight of the ultimate objective of their revolution nor did they compromise on ideological independence. "Our policy," wrote Mao, "is for independence and autonomy within the united front, a policy which is at once for unity and independence."[24] Never once did they cease their persuasive activities of "developing the progressive forces, winning over the intermediate forces and isolating the die-hard forces."[25]

Composition of the united front in terms of "friends" and "foes" necessarily varies from time to time. So far as propaganda policy is concerned, this results in numerous zigzags in operation, but the zigzags are probably mainly for tactical purposes, while certain strategic principles remain both consistent and firm.

Almost immediately after the Communists came to power on the Chinese mainland in 1949, Mao tried to define the Party's friends and foes:

> Except for the imperialists, feudalists, bureaucratic bourgeoisie, Kuomintang reactionaries and their henchmen, all persons are our friends. We have a broad and consolidated revolutionary united front which is so broad that it includes the working class, peasant class, petty bourgeoisie and national bourgeoisie.[26]

Actually, the Communists claim to have only two major enemies: "imperialism" abroad and "feudalism" at home. "Kuomintang reactionaries" and "bureaucratic bourgeoisie" are held responsible for bringing in "imperialism" from abroad and for supporting "feudalism" at home.

So far as the "friends" are concerned, one must remember that they do not all receive the same amount of affection. As early as 1939, Mao pointed out that "the fundamental force of the united front is the working class." The peasantry is considered the "firm ally," the urban petty bourgeoisie a "reliable ally," and the national bourgeoisie is important, Mao points out, only "at the present stage."[27]

Now consider for a moment the implications of the united front for persuasion policies.

The working class, never an important class in traditional China either by numerical strength or political influence, suddenly became the "ruling class" in the Communist society of 1949. Necessarily their "class consciousness" must be raised to the highest level, and they must be educated to assume their new leadership. But a program of thorough indoctrination to acquaint the workers with their new position, new authority, and new responsibilities is not an easy one, and it means that the workers must participate vigorously in various struggles to wrest power and leadership from the bourgeoisie. It is one thing for workers to be pleased with their new position of honor but quite another for them to carry out their new duties and responsibilities. Even after a series of "thought-reform campaigns" in 1952, some workers still said, according to a pro-Communist professor in Shanghai, that "they don't want to have the responsibilities of being the leading class"![28] Even the Communists admit that many workers simply "cannot grasp the full meaning of the slogan 'Be the real master,'" and that others are guilty of *tang chia pu tso chu,* which means "being masters but taking no responsibilities."

The Chinese Communists have an even more complicated problem with the peasants. For years, the Chinese Communists had secretly enjoyed being mistakenly referred to as "harmless land reformers," and it was only natural for the peasants to assume that they, rather than the workers, were to be the main force of the revolution. Even as recently as 1958, after the commune program had been put into effect, Communist propagandists were still combatting the "unthinkably ridiculous thought" that "people's democratic dictatorship should be led by peasants."[29]

There were other serious ideological blocks in the minds of the peasants. During the early stages of the land-reform program, it was not always easy to convince them of the necessity of hating and struggling against the landlord class. Then there were problems of "political conservatism," "irresponsible individualism," the peasants' "religious superstitions and ethics," and a high peasant illiteracy. One can readily see that the Communists have had a formidable task of persuasion to re-indoctrinate and re-educate the peasants.

So far as the petty bourgeoisie is concerned, Mao writes, "They must be won over and attended to because they generally can join and support the revolution and are its good allies." But "their drawback," he continues, "is that some of them are easily influenced by the bourgeoisie; hence it is necessary to pay attention to carrying out revolutionary propaganda and organizational work among them."[30] This is a class of people consisting mainly of intellectuals, small merchants, handicraftsmen, and professionals. Needless to say, the intellectuals are probably the most important element in the group, and, so far as the Communists are concerned, they require the most serious attention from the Party's persuasive activities. Mao comments:

> A section of the intellectuals often leaves the revolutionary ranks at critical moments and becomes passive, while a few may even become enemies of the revolution. The intellectuals can overcome these defects only after they have gone through a long period of mass struggle.[31]

How this "mass struggle" is used as a special form of persuasion and indoctrination is a story by itself and will be discussed in a later chapter.

Then there is the national bourgeoisie, which Mao considers to be "a class with a dual character." He explains:

> On the one hand, this class is oppressed by imperialism and fettered by feudalism and is consequently in contradiction with both. . . . But on the other hand, it lacks the courage to oppose imperialism and feudalism thoroughly because it is economically and politically flabby and its economic ties with imperialism and feudalism are not yet completely severed.[32]

He makes it plain that the national bourgeoisie cannot be a leading class of the united front because "the social and economic status of the national bourgeoisie has determined its feebleness; it lacks foresight, lacks boldness, and in part fears the masses."[33]

To deal with the bourgeoisie as a whole, Mao proposes the method of "uniting, as well as struggling against" it. "Here unity means the united front; struggle means, during the time of unity, 'peaceful' and 'bloodless' ideological and organizational struggle, which will be transformed into an armed struggle when the proletariat is forced to break with the bourgeoisie."[34]

Communist literature is full of discussion on the strategies and tactics of the united front. But two principles seem to have received special attention: (1) "To attract as many people as possible into actual struggle by offering things likely to meet the most urgent needs of the masses and by using the slogans that can most easily be understood by the masses of a certain level of class consciousness at a given place and time." (2) "To help, participate in actively, and lead all revolutionary movements that can contribute to the liberation of the proletariat."[35] These two principles underline not merely the entire scheme of the united front and propaganda but all Communist operations. The list of Communist slogans through the history of the Party is endless, and one has the impression that Marxist disciples are always offering something to some people in some places. There are, of course, such general commodities as democracy, freedom, equality, prosperity, and peace. And there are others. Take, for instance, a slogan that is perhaps most familiar to people in a pre-Communist or non-Communist state: "We must protect wages." Before the Communists took over the Chinese mainland, this was the slogan most loudly shouted and vehemently demanded. But hear the Communist propagandists' explanation:

> It is true that the slogan "We must protect wages" cannot solve any fundamental problems in revolution. But when the workers have not yet reached a high level of class consciousness, this slogan can make the masses gradually realize their interests and to unite together for the struggle. Properly led, they may gradually reach a higher level of consciousness and understand that the protection of wages alone cannot solve their poverty and suffering and that there are things more significant than the protection of wages, i.e., to engage in the anti-capitalist struggle and to overthrow the capitalist authority. It is true that political struggle is far more fundamental than economic struggle. But in certain places and at certain times, the Party has to offer such slogans and lead the people for economic struggle. Otherwise, the Party will be separated from the masses and the masses cannot become revolutionaries.[36]

One no longer hears this slogan in Communist China, where the workers are now supposed to be "the masters of the new society." But this does not necessarily mean that the "new masters" are so perfectly happy with their new role that they have no more complaints. As a matter of fact, a series of incidents in factories and enterprises in China's major cities during 1957 indicated the contrary. But, consistent with the Communist concept of "mass line" and theory of class, an editorial in *Jen Min Jih Pao* shrewdly handled the whole matter by pinning almost the entire blame on "bureaucratic practices" in the enterprises and by scolding the cadres for their "inability" to grasp the "correct method" of "uniting, criticizing, and again uniting" with the masses.[37] One of the major Communist slogans in 1957 was "to handle correctly the internal contradictions among the people." The workers' complaints and threats of strike were not regarded as symptomatic of a conflict among classes but of "conflicts between right ideas and wrong ideas, between partial interests and over-all interests and between immediate interests and long-term interests."

Let us consider another case: The proletariat, as far as Communist strategy is concerned, may sometimes be forced to join hands temporarily with the enemies, but so long as its interests are served, this action can always be justified. This is evidenced in the alternate cooperation and hostility that marked the early relationship between Nationalists and Communists. But let us use an illustration that is perhaps better known in the West.

One hears a good deal about the Communist cries for peace. They are forever engaging in some kind of "peace campaign" or "peace movement." Every year the masses in Communist China are mobilized to participate in campaigns to put their signatures on "petitions," "declarations," or even "oaths" of "peace." For instance, the "peace signature movement" of 1950, the Communists claim, resulted in 223,723,545 signatures between August and November.[38] In 1955, this became the "signature movement opposing use of atomic weapons" and more than 400 million signatures were reported.[39] But what do the Chinese Communists really feel about the "peace movements," either at home or abroad? I quote the Communist propagandists again:

> There are now large-scale, powerful peace campaigns in capitalist countries. Those participating in these campaigns represent all kinds of people, including petty bourgeoisie and even capitalist elements. Although such campaigns are not socialistic in nature, they are against imperialism, the deadly enemy of the working class. The de-

velopment of such campaigns is undoubtedly helpful to the liberation of the working class. Therefore, the Communist Party must
participate in and lead such peace campaigns.[40]

4. Unity of Theory and Practice

One more aspect of the Communist doctrine merits brief discussion here. This concerns the Communist stress on the unity of
theory and practice. "If you want to know the theory and methods
of revolution," declared Mao in his article entitled *On Practice,*
"you must participate in the revolution. . . . All truths are ob-
tained through direct experience."[41] Marxism-Leninism, the Communists repeatedly say, is "truth," and a "universal truth." But,
they hasten to add, it is not a dogma; it is a guide to action.

We cannot at this point go into the details of the Communist
concept of truth and practice. It must suffice to point out here that
Chinese Communism is a kind of "working ideology," which requires everyone under its rule to demonstrate his adherence to
the ideology through action. This is called the "application of
theory to one's own work." While outright opposition to the doctrine is obviously forbidden, mere passive acceptance is equally
unacceptable; to the Communist regime, apathy is a cardinal sin.
Everyone must take part in the *tou cheng* (struggle); ideological
indoctrination and practical action are inseparable.

Thus, it is not enough for a peasant in a land reform movement
to "believe" that he has been "exploited." It is not enough to shout
that he loves Communism, that he despises the landlords and
hates feudalism. He must show in action that he has actually
"benefited" from the wisdom of Marxism-Leninism. This means
that he must "accuse," "attack," or "eliminate" his "reactionary
masters," "pour out his grievances against feudalistic landlords
and oppressive Nationalists," participate actively in the tasks assigned by the cadres, or "contribute" his labor or production to the
government in expression of his "gratitude" to the Communist
Party.

One may wonder at this point whether the objective of Chinese
Communist mass persuasion is to instill in the minds of the people
the "correct" Marxist-Leninist ideology or to coerce a whole range
of acceptable behavior. The doctrine governing the Party's activi-

ties obviously implies that only with the possession of a "correct" ideology or class viewpoint can a person behave "correctly." But it is also definitely implied that only by active participation in the tasks prescribed by the Party can a person hope to grasp the ideology.

The question, then, is whether "correct" thinking is the product of "correct" action, or "correct" action the result of "correct" thinking. A clear-cut answer is not readily available, but some clues are suggested by the very nature of the Communist "faith."

Communism offers a conception of the world and of history in a pseudoscientific form that is capable of expression in a few simple formulas. Everyone can imprint these formulas on his memory, like a catechism, and apply them to every historical situation. With the help of these formulas, one can determine where one stands in history and society—even as one follows the call of the Communist Party to change the world. This is not to suggest that Communism is simple political ideology. On the contrary, it is such a complex philosophy, with such an intricate system, that it is not always easy even for learned scholars to grasp. But Communism in Red China or Soviet Russia is not studied objectively as a political system and ideology, as it is in the West. The Chinese Communists neither desire nor plan to turn each peasant or worker into a student of the works of Marx, Engels, Lenin, Stalin, or Mao. They want only believers in Marxism-Leninism—Marxism-Leninism reduced to a few easy-to-understand formulas. They simply want the people to have faith in these formulas and to translate them into action.[42]

In other words, the faith must be practiced. Hence the process of mass persuasion is always built around one specific central task or another. Each one represents a goal prescribed by the Party, offers an opportunity for the people to unite their faith with practice in an approved manner, adds more realism to the doctrines and dogmas, and attempts to push one step further the people's acceptance of, if not dedication to, the ideology.

Anyone who takes even a casual look at the Communist record since the establishment of the Peking regime in 1949 will immediately realize that for ten years the entire nation has always been engaged in one major mass movement or another, simultaneously with large-scale campaigns for different sections of the population at particular times. To name chronologically only the few that are generally known, there have been the Land Reform movements, *hsueh hsi* (study), Resist-America Aid-Korea, propaganda networks, ideological remolding, "three-anti five-anti," suppression of counterrevolutionaries, mutual cooperatives of production, the Five-Year plans, the agricultural cooperatives, "Hundred Flowers," national reconstruction through austerity and diligence, reform through work, "great leap forward," "general line of socialist development," production of steel and iron, and the people's communes.

The propagandistic importance of these campaigns is not meant to prove that every Communist program serves primarily the ideological function of the Party. That would be to overemphasize the role of mass persuasion. It merely suggests that mass persuasion is always synchronized with every task of the Party and that through the tasks some of the major objectives of mass persuasion are achieved:

> It is always important to grasp every opportunity which can push our revolution one step further. Always give full support to complete one central task, mobilize the broad masses and attract them to the general slogan at the time. We must know that revolution is a mass movement, and that actions of the masses must concentrate only on one or at most a few definite and clearly-expressed objectives. . . . After one central task is completed, replace it with another central task. Substitute one general slogan for another new slogan. This is the forward-going law of revolution. It is also the law of gradually elevating mass consciousness and organizational ability.[43]

Soon after 1949, when land reform was the major program in the nation—to take one example—the People's Government made public its New Marriage Law, and an enormous propaganda campaign was begun to acquaint the nation with this document. For almost two months the mass media were flooded with information and comments about the law; high-ranking officials gave long and serious talks about it; oral agitators went all over the countryside to publicize it; people everywhere, particularly "oppressed women," were mobilized "to take advantage of the law." To a casual observer, it might appear that the Communists were trying their very best to "emancipate" the Chinese women. But the so-called "New Marriage Law" was hardly different in principle from the previous laws of the land on the subject.

The gigantic effort of the Communists to make propaganda regarding the marriage law into a national campaign can only be understood as an effort of mass persuasion for the benefit of other national Party goals. The law was publicized at a time when the Land Reform Movement was the order of the day and when the Party had pledged itself to the elimination of the "reactionary" landlord class and the feudalism it symbolized. The Communist regime was new and peasants and country folk were still conservative, or, as the Communists choose to say, "low in class consciousness" and not "resolute enough to fight against feudalism." So far as the regime was concerned, the problem of gaining support in the masses was a fairly serious one, probably even more serious among the female population in the countryside than among the males. The best way to "wake up" the women would be a program that they could both understand and grasp. The New Marriage Law was such a program.

As everyone knows, many, if not most, Chinese women had long been in a disadvantageous position. "Feudal practices" such as concubinage, matrimonial arrangement by parents, child betrothals, etc., were still fairly common in the rural areas in 1949, despite the fact that the position of women in China then was infinitely better than it had been in earlier Chinese history. By urging the victims of such "feudal practices" to participate in the "new movement of emancipation for women," the Chinese Communists accomplished several tasks at one blow: First, they found a way to mobilize the traditionally conservative Chinese women for aggressive action and thus bring a "turn-over" of classes; second, they gave more substance to the anti-feudalism propaganda; third, they added more realism to the class war; and fourth, they could urge women to take an "active part" in economic production as a symbol of their emancipation from the inequality of the past.

At any rate, the condemnation of the old, feudal values received prominent attention in the propaganda literature concerning the New Marriage Law. Various dramatic accusation meetings or mass struggle meetings were staged to bring out more "grievances" of the people against the "oppressive feudalistic practices." Class struggle was once again the major theme of the campaign, which was simply yet another occasion to educate the masses about the Party line in a different setting.

Shen Chun-ju, then President of the Supreme People's Court, revealed the true propaganda motives of the Party in a nation-wide radio speech:

> How can we guarantee that the Marriage Law be fully and correctly carried out? First, we must engage in propaganda and education among the broad masses of people to make the law understood in every family. . . . So far as the women are concerned, they must understand to break decidedly with the traditional concept of de-pendence, to participate actively in production, to gain economic in-dependence, to engage in political study, to raise the political and cultural level, to learn to work and to take part in all kinds of social construction.[44]

Another example of how the objectives of mass persuasion are achieved is a rather minor campaign in 1958, reported in a four-paragraph news story in *Chinese Literature* (Peking, February, 1959). This campaign called for the compilation of the histories of various factories and plants. It was just one of many campaigns going on in Communist China and does not immediately suggest any direct relevance to mass persuasion. But a closer examination of the story reveals with stark clarity its real propaganda purpose:

> At the beginning of summer, 1958, following the great leap forward in industrial and agricultural production, a flowering of literature and art by the masses, manifested first in folk songs, began unfold-ing in China. At this time, the Union of Chinese Writers proposed that histories of factories and plants be compiled. Workers and em-ployees of factories and mines throughout the country responded warmly and are taking an active part in the compilation. The move-ment spread from Tientsin, Shanghai, Peking, Shenyang [Mukden], Wuhan, Chungking, Canton and other major cities to other parts of the country. This development is of historic cultural significance. For thousands of years, the exploiting classes not only usurped the creations of the labouring people, but also slighted the fact in their histories that these gains were achieved thanks to the people's efforts. History was written as records of feudal monarchies and bourgeois

empires. The creations of the peasants and workers were rarely reflected in history books.

The factory histories will record the development of our industry and the maturing of our working class, and will reflect the richness, the complexity, and the difficulty of these processes. The working class was steeled by hard work and privations and in their struggle against imperialists, capitalists, and all kinds of reactionary forces and ideas. It went through turbulent revolutionary upsurges and suffered years of torment and difficulties under the rule of the Kuomintang White Terror. In writing the history of the factories, the workers will be telling the events of their own plant, some from personal experience. Naturally they are able to do this with great feeling and vividness.

Through the compilation of the factory histories and the exhibitions organized round it, many workers become politically awakened and show more drive in their work. For instance, when the State Textile Mill No. 5, Tientsin, acquainted the workers with the revolutionary traditions of their mill, the workers' sense of responsibility was heightened, and there was a general rise in labour productivity. Many young workers who went to see the exhibition on the mill's history were deeply moved by what they saw of the hardships and struggles of their predecessors in the old society. Some even shed tears. Many workers in factories and mines asked that the histories not only be written into books, but also compiled into pictorial albums or filmed so that the masses of the labouring people can also be politically inspired.

Many sections of society are helping in the compilation of the factory histories. Editors, writers and university history students are going to factories and assisting with writing. In Tientsin alone, histories are being compiled in 200 factories. Literary journals like *People's Literature* of Peking, *New Port* of Tientsin, *Bud* of Shanghai, *Red Rock* of Chungking, *Border Area Literature* of Yunnan, and *Grassland* of Inner Mongolia have recently carried outstanding selections from material already collected for factory histories. Millions are taking part in the compilation of the histories and it is certain that many talented writers will emerge.[45]

Thus far we have discussed four aspects of the Chinese Communist ideology—class consciousness, mass line, united front, and unity of theory and practice—and examined their implications for propaganda policies. Let us now generalize.

Chinese Communism is a class revolution and the key ⟨
the Communist ideology is *tou cheng*, or struggle. A good
munist is supposed to be not only a fearless warrior in the
struggle but also a skillful leader in mobilizing all the peopl— ⏤at
can possibly be united for the struggle. Struggle thus becomes a
normal function of existence. In this struggle, there are friends
to be won over and enemies to be eliminated, hostile ideology to
be eradicated and orthodox ideology to be established, old systems
to be torn down and new systems to be built up, obstructive values
to be uprooted and revolutionary values to be cultivated, con-
tradictory symbols to be condemned and complimentary symbols
to be glorified. This is a struggle that involves everyone under the
Communist rule. It requires the ruling elite to be ideologically
superior to, but intimately united with, the broad masses. It demands both ideological unanimity and behavioral conformity.
Everything in it is believed to be dependent on and determined
by a specially prescribed class consciousness.

In this struggle, persuasion serves a dual function. It acts as a
kind of fuel that provides the driving power of the struggle. It also
acts as a kind of lubricant that helps to smooth the operation. It
is used to inflame as well as to soothe mass emotions in the struggle. It is constantly at work in all feasible vehicles of human expression and every means of communication that influences attitude and behavior.

While no attempt is made here to conduct an organic analysis
of the chemistry of persuasion, it is worthwhile to point out one
particular ingredient that is especially noticeable. This is the psychological element of grievance. It is probably the single most
important power-producing element, serving to generate the necessary heat and energy for the operation of the class struggle.

Since the class struggle must necessarily be based on tensions
between classes, the tensions that exist must be increased, or must
be created where they do not exist. The regime must manufacture
and/or magnify the class antagonism it claims is an integral part
of either "class" or "political" consciousness.

Completely contented human beings are few in the world and
are probably even rarer than usual in China. Political corruption,
economic misery, social injustice, and outworn traditions are

sufficient to produce, with or without external instigation, recalcitrance and anger among the people. When given a proper outlet, those previously suppressed feelings can generate a tremendous amount of energy or power (although they can also lead, as history repeatedly shows, to disastrous or terrifying results). In the hands of the Chinese Communists, persuasion is manipulated to provide such an outlet.

It is no wonder, therefore, that the slogan "To transform grievance into power" has long been hailed as a working formula for mass persuasion in Communist China. Ideologically, this formula has its proper place in the Communist contradiction.[46] Operationally, it finds application in almost every form and phase of Communist persuasion.

Generally speaking, two principles are followed by the Communists to exploit the people's grievances: (1) to transform personal into public or mass hatred; and (2) to transform individual into class hatred. These principles are most noticeable in accusation and *tou cheng* meetings, which are often referred to as "self-education in class consciousness" and the "best, living education to distinguish ideologically among enemies, allies, and ourselves."[47]

> The reason that the accusation meeting is an effective method of educating the masses is because it educates and mobilizes the masses by their own experiences, sufferings and interests. . . . Through the accusation meeting, the masses are able to concentrate their old and new hatreds, to unite their today with tomorrow, to connect their individual interests with the interests of the country, and to understand the greatness of People's China and the preciousness of the new life. . . . Therefore, accusation meetings can educate the masses most deeply and definitely; they can also mobilize the masses most powerfully.[48]

I have made no effort here to spell out specific Communist policies of persuasion in specific details, not because it is an impossible task but because it would be both thankless and meaningless. To examine Communist doctrine for propaganda policies is a far more fruitful approach than to try to nail down their certain special rules. Liu Shao-chi writes: "The organizational forms and methods of work of the Party are determined by the Party's internal and external conditions and by its political tasks, and must be allowed a certain degree of flexibility."[49]

This quotation may remind one of what Goebbels once said: "Propaganda has no policy, it has purpose." This may be too cynical a view to be accepted seriously, but one can certainly agree with Lerner that:

> Propaganda always has some policy. The policy probably will not be made by propagandists, and it probably will not remain forever the same. Since policy is the sequence of governing decisions in any body politic, it is likely to fluctuate through time as changing conditions alter issues and modify alternatives. Although its policy may shift, however, the purpose of propaganda remains constant: to serve that policy with maximum effectiveness.[50]

3. THE BACKGROUND OF MASS PERSUASION

On February 1, 1942, in a lecture on the eradication of "muddled" and "dangerous" ideas, Mao Tse-tung concluded with two methodological principles: (1) "learn from past experience in order to avoid future mistakes" and (2) "treat the illness in order to save the man." He explained:

> We must expose without personal considerations all past errors, analyse and criticise them scientifically so that we will be more careful and do better work in future. This is the meaning of the principle "learn from past experience in order to avoid future mistakes." But in exposing errors and criticising defects, our whole purpose is the same as the doctor's in treating a case; namely, to cure the patient but not to kill him. A person suffering from appendicitis will recover if his appendix is removed by the surgeon. Any person who has committed errors is welcome to treatment until he is cured and becomes a good comrade, so long as he does not conceal his malady for fear of taking medicine or persist in his errors until he becomes incorrigible, but honestly and sincerely wishes to be cured and made better. You cannot cure him by subjecting him to hearty abuse or giving him a sound thrashing. In treating a case of ideological or political illness, we should never resort to violence, but should adopt the attitude of "treating the illness in order to save the man," which alone is the correct and effective method.[1]

Six days later, speaking on certain anti-Marxist ideas and behaviors that are diagnosed as "petty bourgeois ideology," Mao observed that China was a country with a large petty bourgeois class and that many of its members had "joined the Party without shedding their petty bourgeois tails, long or short." Then he offered this clinical approach:

It is not easy to liquidate these things and sweep them clean. We must do it properly; in other words, we must use persuasive reasoning. If our reasoning is persuasive and to the point, it will be effective. In reasoning we must begin by administering a shock and shouting at the patient, "You are ill!" so that he is frightened into a sweat, and then we tell him gently that he needs treatment.[2]

The surgery of tail-shedding turned out to be group therapy. Moreover, the actual act of shedding the tail was to be performed by the patients themselves. Mao's surgical method, as his disciples popularized it later, is described in an embarrassingly unrefined manner in the following words: "to take off your pants in public and to go through the pain of cutting off the tail."[3] In more civilized and understandable terms, this means that the individual applies the method of criticism and self-criticism in group indoctrination to search for, identify, and repudiate his "erroneous" beliefs or ideas.

It is interesting that Mao, with apparently no medical training himself, frequently speaks of the problem of ideological reform in clinical terms. In 1945, emphasizing the importance of the method of criticism and self-criticism he again wrote in hygienic terms:

We have said that a room must be regularly cleaned or dust will accumulate in it, and that our faces must be regularly washed or they will be smeared with dirt. The same is true of our comrades' minds and our Party's work. The proverb "Running water does not go stale and door-hinges do not become worm-eaten" indicates how these things can be ceaseless motion immune from the harmful effects of microbes or other organisms.[4]

He went on to discuss methods "to prevent various kinds of political dust and microbes from producing harmful effects on the minds of our comrades and the physique of our Party."

A few years later, in 1949, when the entire Chinese mainland came under Communist rule, Mao and his followers were not entirely helpless or inexperienced when they came face to face with millions of patients with "petty bourgeois tails." The "political and ideological dust" was thick, heavy, and unhealthy to the Communists. The people, so far as they were concerned, were "plagued by political maladies of various kinds and degrees," and there were also "ideological diseases" both deadly and contagious. Worst of all, many of the patients probably were not even cognizant of their "political illness."

But Mao was determined to have an "ideologically healthy" state and he had his own standard of ideological health. The unsightly "petty bourgeois tails" were to be chopped off. The suffocating political dust was to be swept away. Deadly diseases— some blown over from abroad through the germs of imperialism and colonialism, some developed by the bacteria of feudalism and others caused by the interaction of the two—were to be checked and eliminated. The Communists were to be fortified with heavy doses of the wonder drugs of Marxism-Leninism-Stalinism-Maoism in order to protect themselves from contamination and to engage in the massive ideological clean-up operation in the nation.

Article 41 of the Common Program, the first major policy platform of the Peking regime in 1949, specifies the "eradication of all feudalistic, compradore-like and fascistic ideologies and the development of the ideology of serving the people" as one of the major objectives of all cultural and educational tasks. Using every means of communication, the Communist conquerors informed the nation of the ideological terms, concepts, methods, and attitudes required of the citizen if he were to survive and live healthily in the new order. To those who were considered ideologically ill but not beyond cure, the Communists shouted what they had learned from Mao in the Yenan days: "You are ill." The shock was administered and the patients duly frightened into a sweat, until they reached the point of baring their ideological malady and expressing their wishes to be cured. Treatment was then offered. Thus began nationwide therapy on a monumental scale.

The clinical approach, though of a slightly different variety, was also applied to members of the proletarian class. These were not people born with "petty bourgeois tails" or "ideological fraility." But they were not immune to imperialistic germs and feudalistic bacteria which had been "poisoning" the air for centuries. Many had become so accustomed to the "poisonous" air they breathed that their "natural instinct" for socialist living might have been impaired, the Communists reasoned. As masters of the new society, these people were entitled to a new bill of ideological health. They were to learn the new rules of ideological hygiene in the new state of people's democracy. They were to take revenge and "settle the account" with those who had sought to "corrupt and poison" their minds. Their class consciousness was to be nursed and developed to the degree that it would not only serve as an antiseptic against all corrupting elements but would also bring to life their fighting instinct for revolution.

To go on with this clinical metaphor would be tedious, but it is important to make clear that it is not at all infrequent in Chinese Communist literature, either before or after 1949. In this study, our purpose is to examine the nature of the massive ideological remolding and "cleansing" movement in China since 1949. But before doing so, there is one important question to be answered: How did the Chinese Communists come to this concept of total ideological reform? What is the history behind the whole phenomenon of mass ideological reform in Communist China?

•The Background

The subtlety and skill with which the Chinese Communists approach thought reform—as revealed particularly in their handling of the American prisoners of war and of Chinese intellectuals—have often led people to wonder where, when, and how the Marxists learned or acquired their methods and techniques. They appear as such veterans of what seem to be psychiatric and psychoanalytical practices that one could even suspect that they had read Freud and Jung along with Marx and Lenin in their early revolutionary days. But there is no evidence that they did so. A reasonably good guess is that the Chinese Communists have acquired their knowledge of ideological reform from three other major sources.

The first and easily most important source is the Chinese Communists' actual experience in the years when they fought for the acquisition of power. For a generation and more, their tasks had largely been insurrectional. Their political, even military, work had been mainly propaganda and agitation, and they were naturally involved with the mobilization, organization, and indoctrination of both the masses and their own Party members. It is likely that many of their tricks of the trade were learned through trial and error.

The second source is the Soviet Union. It is difficult to determine when the operational, not just ideological or theoretical, principles of the Russian experience of revolution were introduced to and practiced by the Chinese Marxists. Chinese Communist literature is flooded with testaments to the inspiration and wisdom of the Soviet experience for nearly everything done in China. But these statements are often expressions of sentiment rather than fact. It is worth noting, however, that the works of Lenin and Stalin constituted a major part of the required readings of the Chinese Communists in their Yenan days and later, and that certain methods regarding ideological matters were modified and then applied to Chinese conditions.

Take, for example, the method of criticism and self-criticism. A Chinese booklet on this very subject, entitled *On Self-Criticism*,[5] contains seven articles of which only two are taken from Chinese newspapers; the other five are all Soviet. They include: Stalin, "On Self-Criticism"; Stalin, "To Oppose Vulgarizing Self-Criticism"; Lenin, "On Our Newspapers"; A. A. Zhdanov, "Concerning Criticism and Self-Criticism"; and the "Resolutions of the Eighth National Congress of the Bolsheviks Concerning the Soviet Newspapers and Publications."

Let us take another example. Shortly after the Communists came to power in China, they selected twelve books as required reading for their cadres' ideological training. Out of the twelve books, three are by Marx and Engels; most of the rest are from the writings of Lenin, Stalin and Soviet writers; only a few articles by Chinese Communists are included. Not one volume consists entirely or mostly of writings by Chinese Communists.[6]

The third source can be loosely referred to as the accumulated political and cultural experience of the Chinese. This is clearly and frequently revealed in the writings of Mao Tse-tung, who quotes Chinese proverbs and maxims with both ease and dexterity. Manipulation of persuasive media and techniques as instruments of control, one can be sure, is not an invention of the Communists. Mencius probably realized the value of persuasion when he remarked: "When men are subdued by force, they do not submit in their minds, but only because their strength is inadequate." Even an illiterate Chinese can repeat the old saying, "Submission by mouth is not nearly as desirable as submission by heart." (*Kuo Fu Pu Yu Hsin Fu.*) In fact, the whole history of Chinese culture is full of examples that suggest rich analytic insights into the study of minds. For instance, the simple Chinese expression *tsun hsi tso jen*, or "to become a new man," involves a whole set of complex theories of personality, identity, and ego identification in psychology, psychiatry, and psychoanalysis.

Perhaps the most convenient way to understand the background of ideological reform is to examine the role of political indoctrination in the growth of the Chinese Communist Party. The focus of attention here must be placed on the contributions of Mao Tsetung. While it is difficult to determine how much of what has been going on in China is actually Mao's blueprint, there is every reason to believe that he, more than anyone else in the Party, has given serious attention to the matter of political indoctrination.

A general practice of historians, Communists and others alike, is to divide the history of the Chinese Communist Party into four periods: (1) the early beginnings of the Party from 1921 to 1927; (2) the period of the Chinese Soviet Government and the well-known Long March from 1928 to 1935; (3) the period of the Yenan Government, anti-Japanese war, and the Party's acquisition of power from 1936 to 1949; and (4) the period of the People's Government of China since 1949.

1921–27

It is doubtful that the experience during the early period of the Chinese Communist Party contributed much of significance to the regime's knowledge of ideological indoctrination. At that time, the Party was under the control of Chen Tu-hsiu and Li Ta-chao, both intellectuals and political thinkers whose greatest influence was on other intellectuals, but both of whom had little to do with the kind of agitation work now common in Communist China; neither had much contact with the masses. Chen was later condemned by the Party as a rightist, and his contributions to the Party were not only minimized but ridiculed. Li, executed by the warlord Chang Tso-lin in 1927, died too early to be credited with an important role in the indoctrination activities of the Party.

Furthermore, the Party was, during this period, actually no more than the leftist wing of the revolutionary movement dominated by the Nationalist Party. Like the Kuomintang members, the Communists were often ideologically confused and politically inexperienced. While both engaged in intensive propaganda activities, they were quite unsophisticated and amateurish in comparison with contemporary practices elsewhere.

It is important to note that although Mao was not a leading figure in the Party in this period, he was, to use a Communist expression, "intimately united with the masses." His work was primarily propaganda and agitation; this gave him probably his first taste of insurrectional politics.

Mao was extremely active in politics while he was a student at a normal school in Hunan and apparently formed a number of organizations, including the *Hsin Min* study group in 1917. He also organized a Marxist study group in Hunan in 1920, shortly after such groups were formed by Chen Tu-hsiu and Li Ta-chao in Peking. When the Party was organized in 1921, Mao was already a veteran organizer of workers in his native province, which was then no haven for revolutionaries.

If the official biographies of Mao Tse-tung are in any way reliable, Mao had acquired rich experience in propaganda and agitation during this time. Many of his activities became common practice in later periods—political publications of various kinds and forms, wall newspapers, discussion groups, night schools or literacy classes for workers and peasants, "self-study universities," "youth corps," training of revolutionary functionaries, mass demonstrations, union work, and a host of others.[7] Mao's official biographers even lead one to believe that some of the most fundamental concepts of Chinese Communist ideological indoctrination were already in Mao's mind. He was credited, for instance, with the following statement written in 1919 to protest the arrest of Chen Tu-hsiu: "The most important problem of China today is not the civil war among warlords; it is how to elevate the political consciousness of the people to a higher level."[8] His article, entitled "Unity of the Masses" and published in the *Hsiang Kiang Review*—one of the magazines published and edited by Mao in 1919—was hailed by his biographers as the first evidence of his policy of the "united front," one of the Party's most important doctrinal principles. While it is both obvious and natural that Mao's role in the Party during this early period is dramatized and exaggerated, it is at least true that Mao was much closer to the reality of revolution and insurrectional politics than either Chen or Li. He did go through the apprenticeship of propaganda and agitation work; he was not yet a military leader and had no chance to succeed either by coercion or by violence. Several warlords had put a price on his head. He needed supporters and sympathizers for his own survival, if not for the revolution. Persuasion was his only weapon, and Mao made maximum use of it.

Mao's approach to ideological problems was therefore a practical one, a result of circumstances rather than choice. A young man of peasant origin, a graduate of normal school, he had neither the equipment nor the opportunity to engage in a theoretical study of Marxism-Leninism on a high intellectual level. He was close to peasants, workers, and students of his own kind, and he went about his political work in his own unsophisticated but apparently effective manner. His successes undoubtedly excited him; they also led him to the point of no return. His experience hardened his class bitterness, added reality to the problem of revolution, and, as we shall see later, taught him many practical lessons on working with peoples' minds and thoughts.

1927–35

This period covers the years from Mao's emergence as a political and military leader to his establishment in Yenan following the Long March.

Mao's early experience among peasants and workers paid off handsomely, and almost immediately, in 1927, when he wrote his now widely publicized article entitled "Report on the Investigation of the Peasants' Movement in Hunan."[9] It was with both experience and conviction that he urged the establishment of "peasants' associations" as the "best means of engaging in political propaganda." He asked: "Can ten thousand schools of law and politics hope to popularize political education in the countryside as much as the peasants' associations can accomplish in political education in a relatively short time?" His answer: "I don't think so."

> To use those simple slogans, pictures and speeches for political propaganda is like sending every one of the peasants to a political school. The success is big and great. According to our comrades in the countryside, political propaganda was quite thoroughly done in the three recent mass meetings: anti-British demonstration, anniversary of October Revolution, and celebration of the Northern Expedition. In places where peasants associations are set up, such mass meetings have popularized quite effectively our political propaganda and mobilized into action whole villages. We should in the future make use of all opportunities to enrich the content of the simple slogans and to make their meaning better understood gradually.[10]

In the same article, Mao also wrote approvingly of a number of available methods of "attacking the landlords politically." It is interesting how many of these methods were used later in the Land Reform Movement "to sharpen the class consciousness of the peasants." To list just a few:

> *To Settle the Account.* . . . "Committees on Settling Accounts" are set up in many places to deal mainly with local villains and bullies, who usually tremble at the sight of such organizations. Such account-settling movement is quite popular in various towns. The significance is not to get back the money (alleged to have been misused by them), but to expose the crimes of the villains and bullies and thus to crash and collapse their political and social position.
>
> *Small-scale interrogation.* When there are those who commit the minor offense of insulting or obstructing the policies and actions of the peasant associations, get a group to go to their homes and start questioning. Let such people write down their repentance and write down their promise that they will never try to damage the reputation of peasant associations.
>
> *Mass demonstration.* Lead an army of people for a demonstration against those villains and bullies who have antagonized the peasant associations. Have meals in their houses, butcher a few pigs and get their rice. . . . Recently a group of 15,000 was led to accuse six bullies. The demonstration lasted four days, and more than 130 heads of pigs were butchered. . . .
>
> *Parade with high hats.* The villains and bullies were each given a

paper-made high hat on which their crimes were given. They were led with a rope with large groups of people around them. Gongs were sounded and flags were raised high in order to attract public attention. Such punishment frightened the villains and bullies most. . . . One peasant association was especially skillful in handling such a parade. A local bully was captured and he was told to wear a high hat in parade. He was so scared that his face turned green. But the association passed a resolution not to give him the high hat on that particular day. . . . The bully went home but he never did know on which day he was to wear the high hat. He was so worried at home that he couldn't sit or sleep.[11]

It did not take Mao long to realize the necessity of ideological education, after he had engaged in armed rebellion against the government. On November 25, 1928, hardly a year after the birth of the Red Army, Mao wrote an article reviewing the battle of Chingkanshan, near Kiangsi and Hunan.[12] Of the six reasons he gave for the defeat in this battle, three dealt with ideological indoctrination. A number of his observations had an important bearing on his later approach to ideological work:

1. He emphasized "political education" and demanded "class consciousness" for all officers and soldiers of the Red Army.

2. He discovered that "the most effective method of propaganda toward the enemies is to release prisoners of war [after propaganda work] and to give treatment to wounded soldiers."

As soon as we captured the enemy soldiers and officers, we engaged in propaganda work and then divided them into two groups: those who wanted to stay, and those who wanted to leave. Those who wanted to leave were given money for travel. This is the best way to fight against the enemy propaganda that "Red bandits kill everyone they find." Our Red Army soldiers would offer comfort and arrange farewell parties for the prisoners of war with enthusiasm. In every "Farewell Meeting for New Brothers," prisoners gave speeches to express their gratitude.[13]

It was probably no coincidence that similar practices were reported by U. S. prisoners of war in Korea.

3. He realized the necessity of purge in the Party. He complained about the large number of "opportunists" who joined the Party during the "high tide of revolution" in June, 1928. These

were the people who, he said, did not receive adequate Party indoc-trination and betrayed the Party later. In September of 1928, Mao took drastic action to "purify the membership of the Party." He did not call the campaign "ideological remolding," as he did in 1942; he called it *hsi tang,* or to "wash the Party."[14]

4. He began to notice symptoms of "dangerous and erroneous thoughts" operating against the Party and he showed signs of im-patience with the "petty bourgeois ideology." He complained:

> This year, opportunism within the Party still exists. Some of our Party members have lost their will to fight. . . . Others are aggres-sive but they are inclined to be interested in blind insurrection. These are all reflections of petty bourgeois ideology. Such conditions after long-time struggle and Party education, are gradually decreas-ing. But in the Red Army such petty bourgeois ideas still exist.[15]

All these ideas were crystallized in Mao's mind when he wrote a long article in December, 1929, to summarize the existing "er-roneous thoughts and ideas" within the Party and to suggest methods of correction.[16] Here he opened fire against the "simple-minded military viewpoint," "revolutionary impatience," "military mercenary mentality," "ultrademocratic viewpoint," "anti-organi-zation mentality," "absolute equalitarianism," "subjectivism," "in-dividualism," "bandit mentality," "sectarianism," and "adventur-ism." He had a ready explanation for all such "erroneous ideas":

> The various incorrect ideas within the Party in the Red Fourth Army are caused by the fact that people with peasant and petty bourgeois background have formed the absolute majority of the Party's fundamental organization and that the leading authorities of the Party have failed to engage in a resolute struggle against such erroneous ideas and to offer the Party members an adequate educa-tion and indoctrination.[17]

Since military action appeared to be the major task at the time, Mao cautioned his followers: "The Red Army fights not for the sake of fighting but for the sake of carrying on propaganda among the masses, organizing the masses, arming the masses, and helping the masses to set up a revolutionary regime." It apparently pained Mao to see his followers overlook the political and ideological mis-sion of the Red Army.

There is no need to go into all of Mao's suggestions on dealing with "erroneous ideas." It is significant to note, however, that he singled out the method of criticism as one of the best tools for, particularly, destroying "petty bourgeois individualism" and "subjectivism." The term *ssu hsiang tou cheng*, or "ideological struggle," a watchword of the Peking regime since 1949, was used emphatically in this article.

In studying the writings of Mao before the 1930's, one is left with the impression that he was deeply concerned with the problem of propaganda, agitation, and ideological reform, and that he was constantly experimenting with methods or techniques of political persuasion. But one must not be misled into believing that what has gone on in China since 1949 is only a repetition of what Mao did earlier on a small scale, or that Mao alone made all the contributions to the regime's theoretical and methodological principles. Mao did not, at that earlier time, have full control of the Party, which had just passed from the hands of Chen Tu-hsiu to Li Li-san in 1930. (Li was in power rather briefly and was challenged by Chu Chiu-pai, later executed by the Nationalists in 1935. The real leaders from 1930 to 1935 were Chen Shao-yu [alias Wang Ming] and Ching Pang-hsien [alias Po Ku], both regarded as leaders of the "Moscow-returned students clique.")

We make this brief reference to the historical background of the Party in order to suggest that there were others besides Mao who contributed to its arsenal of techniques for mass persuasion. In spite of their political differences, these leaders were all engaged in insurrectional politics and all had to depend on coercive and persuasive indoctrination to accomplish their objectives. Li particularly distinguished himself in labor organization. Unlike Mao, who was, with Chu Teh, establishing a firm political and military basis in the countryside, Li was busy in political work among workers and other urban groups. With this somewhat different "audience," he naturally had his own fashion of propaganda and agitation.

Even if one agrees with Mao that Li, Chen, Ching, and their followers were entirely wrong politically, and thus that nothing they did contributed to the Chinese Communist revolution, it is at least true that Mao and those in his camp gained profound knowledge and experience in recognizing, understanding, and combatting incompatible ideologies and thoughts. The entire period, with all its intrigues and schemes, provided an advanced working seminar on political indoctrination and ideological struggle for everyone concerned.

While this intricate political fight was going on within the Party between 1929 and 1935, Mao and Chu were busily broadening their political and military influence, under the constant threat of "annihilation" by Chiang Kai-shek and his Nationalists. At the time of the famous Long March in 1934, not only was their political future at stake, but so was their survival. As their revolutionary work became increasingly difficult, the need for effective coercive and persuasive indoctrination became more acute, and their task of propaganda and agitation an ever-increasing challenge. When the Long March was over, Mao recalled proudly and fondly that it was "a manifesto, a propaganda-agitation corps, and a seeding-machine."[18]

As a "manifesto," wrote Mao, the Long March "proclaims to the world that the Red Army is an army of heroes, and that the imperialists and their jackals, Chiang Kai-shek and his kind, are perfect nonentities." As a propaganda-agitation corps, "it declares to the approximately 200 million people of eleven provinces that only the road of the Red Army leads to their liberation." Finally, as a seeding-machine, "It has sown many seeds in eleven provinces, which will sprout, grow leaves, blossom into flowers, bear fruit, and yield a harvest in the future."

But the participants in the Long March were not the only warriors in the political and ideological war of revolution. Leftist artists and writers in the big cities and cultural centers—not all of them Communists—also did their part to popularize the ideas of Marxism-Leninism and the cause of the Chinese Communist Party. And this is an area of "ideological revolution" and persuasive communications where the Communists have always been vigorously active.

1936–49

When the Long March ended in Shensi in 1935, a new era of the Chinese Communist Party began. After defeating the "rightist"

Chang Kuo-tao, who had ruled the Party from 1935 to 1936, Mao quickly and firmly established himself as the leader of the Party.

The policy and tasks of propaganda, agitation, and indoctrination began to take a different turn as a result of circumstances. For the first time in the history of the Party, the Communists began to have a fairly stable base of operation. To win over, indoctrinate, and organize the people under Communist rule was the immediately most important task. Agitation for production was the order of the day, since the Yenan territory was not known for its abundance of agricultural products. Consolidation of the Party was both necessary and urgent.

An even more challenging task of propaganda and agitation presented itself at the outbreak of the Sino-Japanese War in July, 1937. About seven months earlier, Chiang Kai-shek had been forced to accept the Communist "united front" policy against Japan, following the well-known Sian Incident in December, 1936. The cooperation between the Nationalists and Communists, if it ever existed, widened the scope of Yenan's political work and offered new opportunities, new missions, and new problems in mass persuasion.

It is not the purpose of this study to analyze all the twists and turns of policy that the Chinese Communist Party underwent during this period in order to enlarge their political influence. Many able historians have already discussed this phase of the Communist revolution, which is characterized by the Party's loud cries of "united front against Japan," "cessation of civil war," and "realization of the policy of agrarian reform." We shall focus our attention here only on the problems that directly bear on the background of China's present system of mass persuasion.

Now reflect for a moment on the problems of the Party in the realm of ideological indoctrination. There was, first of all, the problem of unifying the Party ideologically. Various kinds of "leftist" and "rightist" ideologies, looking at it from Mao's viewpoint, were prevailing within the Party. There was not only the problem of "petty bourgeois mentality" but also the problem of "peasant conservatism."[19] The level of understanding of Marxism-Leninism, Mao complained, was woefully low among Party members, and their general educational level was perhaps even lower.

Then there was the problem of preparing, both ideologically and functionally, large numbers of cadres to carry out a wide variety of tasks within the Communist-Nationalist coalition. Mao wrote about the policy of "independence and autonomy within the united front," a policy "which is at once for unity and independence."[20] He was speaking not only of political but of ideological independence. Determined that his "cooperation" with the Nationalists would not result in "amalgamation," he scorned the slogan of "Everything through the united front."[21] A thorough prior indoctrination of the cadres and a constant effort to keep them on their toes politically and ideologically once they were at their jobs—both these were essential. Mao repeatedly warned his followers "not to forfeit political objectives" of the Party in their cooperation with the Nationalists and insisted on "the unity in ideology and strictness of discipline of Party members."[22]

Most important of all, there was the immense task of propaganda and agitation among the masses of the Chinese people. The prestige of Chiang Kai-shek and his party was probably at its zenith at this time, and the word "Communism" prompted fear if not resentment in many sectors of the population. The workers and peasants, considered by the Communists to be "naturally inclined" to the Marxist-Leninist doctrine, were probably as ignorant of, and even as hostile to, the whole concept of Communism as were other classes. Curiously enough, Communist sympathizers at the time were not, in general, the proletariat, but intellectuals with "petty bourgeois tails, short and long."

These three problems—ideological purge within the Party, intensified indoctrination and education of Party members and cadres, and propaganda-agitation work among the masses—were of course interrelated. They were all designed to "raise the level of class consciousness" of the different groups of people concerned. There is no doubt that these problems were much in Mao's mind (he wrote on them frequently during this period), for they were all three germane to his plans for the eventual realization of socialism in the country. In May, 1937, Mao described them thus:

> We advocate the theory of the continuous development of revolution, of the continuous development of a democratic revolution into a socialist revolution. The democratic revolution will undergo several

stages of development, all under the slogan of a democratic republic. It is a long process of struggle from the hegemony of the bourgeoisie to the hegemony of the proletariat, a process of winning leadership, which depends on the condition that the Communist Party raises the level of consciousness and organization of the proletariat, the level of consciousness and organization of the peasantry and the urban petty bourgeoisie.[23]

He went on to say:

The staunch ally of the proletariat is the peasantry, and next to it, the urban petty bourgeoisie. It is the bourgeoisie that will dispute with us for hegemony. . . . It depends on the strength of the masses and on our correct policies to overcome the vacillation and the lack of thoroughness of the bourgeoisie; otherwise the bourgeoisie will turn round to overcome the proletariat.[24]

That Mao should be suspicious of the bourgeoisie was natural. But what was unusual, and what distinguished Mao and his followers from other Party leaders at the time, was a specific and pragmatic policy toward the bourgeoisie:

It is a Trotskyite approach, with which we cannot agree, to reject the participation of the bourgeoisie in the revolution because it can only be temporary and to describe the alliance with the anti-Japanese section of the bourgeoisie (in a semi-colonial country) as capitulationism. Such an alliance today is precisely a bridge that has to be crossed on our way to socialism.[25]

To cross that bridge safely, Mao trusted in his weapon of ideological struggle. Even a casual review of Mao's works will reveal that he has used this weapon ceaselessly and skillfully. It should be clear to the reader that what the Chinese Communist Party did later to the bourgeoisie, after the harsh "three-anti five-anti," "Hundred Flowers," and various "ideological remolding" campaigns, was no coincidence but the accurate reflection of a long-standing policy of Mao and his disciples. For the primary element in the ideological purge of the Party during this early period concerned the eradication of bourgeois ideologies and practices.

Ideological purge, in the Communist idiom, means "internal Party struggle" or "ideological struggle." Now this period of the Chinese Communist Party, from 1936 to 1949, began with Mao's

successful struggle against Chang Kuo-tao's "right opportunism."
Although little Communist literature is available describing the
actual details of the struggle, Mao's work frequently reveals that
the struggle was not handled lightly in the Pasi meeting of 1935
and the Yenan meeting of 1937.[26] Mao admitted later that the lessons learned and achievements made at the meetings "supply the
prerequisites for us to unite the Party from now on, to strengthen
its ideological, political, and organizational unity."[27] The method
of criticism and self-criticism was used extensively to eradicate
"unhealthy thoughts" in the Party. While it is difficult to determine
what degree of physical purges was involved in these struggles,
"ideological purification of the Party membership" through "democratic" methods appeared, at least, to be the main objective. Mao
summarized these experiences by remarking that, "In the last sev-
enteen years (1921–38), our Party has in general learned to use
the Marxist-Leninist weapon of ideological struggle to combat incorrect ideas within the Party on two fronts—right opportunism as
well as left opportunism."[28]

The situation in China in the late 1930's did not permit Mao or
his followers to give undivided attention to the ideological purge
of the Party, for there were other pressing problems. One very urgent one concerned the cadres:

> To guide a great revolution there must be a great party and many
> excellent cadres [Mao wrote in 1937]. . . . The organization of
> our Party must be expanded throughout the country; it must pur-
> posefully train tens of thousands of cadres and several hundreds of
> excellent mass leaders. These cadres and leaders must understand
> Marxism-Leninism, they must have political insight and ability to
> work, they must be full of spirit of self-sacrifice, capable of solving
> problems independently; and they must remain firm in the midst of
> difficulties and work loyally and devotedly for the nation, the class
> and the Party.[29]

The Party's responsibility, Mao wrote one year later, was "to organize the cadres, nurture them, take good care of them, and make
proper use of them."[30] It was not merely a problem of mobilization
or recruitment. It was mainly a problem of political indoctrination.
"Once the correct political line has been determined, the cadres

will become the decisive factor. Hence to rear large numbers of new cadres according to plan is our fighting task."

Mao suggested five methods to "take care of cadres." Among them were that of giving "guidance," that of "raising their theoretical understanding and working ability to a higher level," and that of "persuasion toward cadres who have erred." In educating and preparing the new and non-Party cadres, members were urged to "get rid of insolent aloofness" and to help the new recruits in every possible way, and were lectured on the "method of persuasion" and the importance of Party solidarity.

There is every reason to believe that, in the process of eliminating incompatible ideologies and establishing a "correct political line" within the Party, Mao and his close associates had to undergo considerable soul-searching themselves. The results of their efforts are evident in Mao's writings, where he tried painfully to instill in the minds of the Party members and cadres his interpretation of Marxism-Leninism-Stalinism, as well as his method of adopting the doctrine to the Chinese situation, and called on the entire Party "to raise the level of understanding of Marxism-Leninism":

So far as the people shouldering the main responsibilities of leadership are concerned, if there are in our Party one to two hundred comrades who have acquired a knowledge of Marxism-Leninism, which is systematic and not fragmentary, practical and not abstract, the fighting capacity of our Party will be greatly heightened and our work in defeating Japanese imperialism will be accelerated. . . .

To turn Marxism into something specifically Chinese, to imbue every manifestation of it with Chinese characteristics, i.e., to apply it in accordance with China's characteristics, becomes a problem which the whole Party must understand and solve immediately.[31]

Mao's solution to the problem was a rigorous program of *hsueh hsi*, or study. He suggested:

All those members of the Communist Party who are fairly qualified to study must study the theory of Marx, Engels, Lenin and Stalin, the history of our nation, and the circumstances and trends of the present movement; moreover, with these comrades as the intermediary, we must organise education for Party members whose cultural level is relatively low. In particular, cadres should study the above-mentioned subjects with attention; members of the Central Committee and senior cadres should especially intensify their study.[32]

But this was no ordinary study, and the process of acquiring knowledge was not simply a matter of reading a few books. The first objective was to "establish the correct attitude toward study." "The enemy of our study," warned Mao, "is self-complacency; anyone who wants really to learn something must first of all get rid of self-complacency." Another objective was to integrate the doctrinal knowledge learned with the work to do. This was what Mao called "unity of theory and practice." The significant point here is that the goal of studying Marxism-Leninism was not to acquire "bookish knowledge"—something despised and condemned in Chinese Communist circles—but to instill in the minds of the members an operational doctrine. (The slogans introduced by Mao at this time were: (1) "To learn without satiety," which suggested the permanency of the program; and (2) "To teach without weariness," which is a famous Confucian expression given a new twist that implied the desired continuous effect of persuasion.)

A special Party journal called *The Communist* was introduced in 1939 to guide the study of Party members and cadres. In his introductory remarks to the journal, Mao emphasized once again that the task was "to help to build up a bolshevised Chinese Communist Party of nation-wide scope and broad mass character, fully consolidated ideologically, politically, and organisationally."[33]

Shortly after this, another journal, called *The Chinese Worker,* was published as "a school for educating the workers and training cadres from among the workers."[34] There were other journals for Party members and cadres in general and for specific educational and ideological levels.

It is interesting to note, however, that a major item of study, emphasized in Mao's remarks about the journals and in other of his writings at the time, concerned the bourgeoisie. Mao took great pains to attack those who opposed the participation of the bourgeoisie; he condemned this as "left closed-door sectarianism." At the same time, he vehemently warned his followers to be on guard against "the mistake of identifying the programme, policy, ideology, practice, etc., of the proletariat with those of the bourgeoisie":

> Such a mistake consists in ignoring the fact that the bourgeoisie (especially the big bourgeoisie) is making every effort to exert its influence not only on the petty bourgeoisie and the peasantry but also on the proletariat and the Communist Party; to destroy the ideological, political and organisational independence of the proletariat and the Communist Party, to turn the proletariat and the Communist Party into an appendage of its own and of its political parties, and to ensure that a group or a political party belonging to its own class reaps all the fruits of the revolution; and it also consists in ignoring the fact that the bourgeoisie (especially the big bourgeoisie) will actually betray the revolution at the moment when the revolution conflicts with the self-interest of such a group or political party. To overlook this aspect is Right opportunism.[35]

Along with Mao, important Communist leaders such as Liu Shao-chi, Chen Yun, and many others took an active part in the ideological training of Party members. For instance, Liu's article "On the Training of a Communist Party member," written in 1939, and Chen's article "How to be a Communist Party Member," also written in 1939, followed Mao's political line almost exactly and emphasized many of the same points.

A variety of political schools or classes were organized at the same time to train Party members and cadres. Among them was the well-known Anti-Japanese Political and Military Academy, commonly known as the Red Academy at Yenan. There were schools for artists, writers, and political cadres; there were literacy classes and schools for peasants, workers, and others at a lower educational level. Essentially, the same things were stressed in the different schools, although the manner of presentation varied. A consistent feature of instruction and indoctrination was criticism and self-criticism.

It is difficult to determine how successful the Chinese Communists were in this study program for ideological indoctrination, because writings of the Communist leaders in the late 1930's reveal their intentions rather than what they actually accomplished. Apparently, however, the study programs did not result in the level of ideological achievement that Mao had anticipated. For this reason, then, the first and major *Cheng Feng,* or "ideological remolding," campaign of the Chinese Communist Party began.

The Cheng Feng Campaign

It is generally agreed that the *Cheng Feng* campaign was started officially on February 1, 1942, when Mao delivered the speech "Rectify the Party's Style in Work" at the Inauguration of the Central Party School at Yenan. It was followed eight days later by another entitled "Oppose the Party 'Eight-Legged Essay,' " delivered at a cadres' meeting in Yenan. And three months later, Mao gave yet another, entitled "Talks at the Yenan Forum on Art and Literature," which was to form the guide to the Party's cultural work from then on.

But the idea of "ideological remolding" was already there in Mao's speech "Reform Our Study," given at a cadres' meeting in Yenan in May, 1941. At any rate, this article is cited by the editors of the *Selected Works of Mao Tse-tung* as the first important *Cheng Feng* document.

> In these articles a forward step was made in summing up past differences over the Party line from the point of view of ideology and analysing the petty bourgeois ideology and petty bourgeois style of work which, masquerading as Marxism-Leninism, were very prevalent in the Party—notably the subjectivist and sectarian tendencies and their form of expression, the Party's "eight-legged essay." He [Mao] urged that a style in work according to the ideological principles of Marxism-Leninism, should be carried out throughout the Party. His call immediately started a great debate inside and outside the Party on proletarian ideology versus petty-bourgeois ideology, and consolidated the position of the former, thus raising considerably the ideological level of the broad section of the cadres and enabling the Party to achieve unprecedented unity.[36]

The method of study used in the *Cheng Feng* campaign, according to Lu Ting-i, now director of the Party's Department of Propaganda, "is the most effective that is proven by history":

> This is a method of study that requires a thorough grasp of several fundamental Marxist-Leninist documents. These documents are used as a basis for one to investigate his own thoughts, to engage in criti-

cism and self-criticism, to analyze the correct and erroneous elements in his own thoughts, to study their composition, to discover the reasons, environment, and sources of their growth and development, to work out the practical methods of correcting the mistakes and to write down one's conclusions of study.[37]

The method is almost identical to the one used in the various ideological remolding campaigns conducted against artists, writers, and intellectuals from 1949 to 1959.

The most famous single case in the campaign of 1942, that of Wang Shih-wei, a Communist writer who became the target of a dramatic and severe "ideological struggle," illustrates vividly the brand of "bourgeois individualism and liberalism" that the Communist Party was determined to eradicate, and the type of "unstable elements" it wished to re-educate.

Wang had joined the Chinese Communist Party in 1926 and had written extensively on and done translations of Marxism-Leninism. The immediate cause for the vehement campaign against him were his two short essays, *"Tsa Wen,"* or "Miscellaneous Essays," and *"Yeh Pai Ho Hua,"* or "The Wild Lily."[38] The Communist version of Wang's "sins" was reported in the official *Chinese Literature* in 1958, shortly after the famous "Hundred Flowers" campaign of 1957:

Wang Shih-wei's slander of the revolutionary camp dealt with the relationship between the leaders and the rank and file. In the *Wild Lily,* he accused Chinese revolutionaries of being contaminated with the "filth of old China," and of "spreading germs and infecting other people." . . . He tried to disrupt unity by claiming that the leaders had "no love" for their subordinates. By making out that the men in responsible positions were heartless hypocrites, Wang tried to stir up feeling among the "youngsters lower down." He said: "The great majority of them have come by devious ways and after painful struggle to Yenan. In the past they knew very little 'love and warmth,' but plenty of 'hate and coldness.' . . . Because they come to Yenan in search of warmth and beauty, they cannot help complaining when they see its ugliness and coldness." . . . But according to him, although the young people complained, the men in power were too stubborn to change. Instead he made them justify themselves by arguments actually made up by Wang Shih-wei: "As our camp exists in the old, dark society, there is bound to be darkness here too. This comes of necessity." He therefore concluded: "If we let such things go on of necessity, the revolution must necessarily fail." . . .

Of course there were petty-bourgeois and bourgeois intellectuals who faltered in the face of difficulties or demanded absolute equality and "warmth." That was why Wang Shih-wei posed as their champion to stir up feeling against the Party among the rank and file of revolutionary workers, and tried to turn young people into his tools. He argued that if certain older revolutionaries with heavy responsibilities had slightly better living conditions than the average, this was undemocratic and they were a privileged class. One could see plainly that if the absolute equalitarianism typical of small landowners' ideology develops unchecked, a point will be reached when nobody is allowed to ride a horse and no casualty has a prior claim to a stretcher. If this goes far enough, the revolution is indeed doomed.

Similarly all Wang's talk of "love" and "warmth" was another trick to make petty-bourgeois and bourgeois intellectuals discontented and stir up hatred for the Party and Party leadership. In this way he hoped to drive a wedge through the revolutionary ranks.[39]

This account of the incident does not actually reveal some of Wang's harshest remarks, such as the following:

He [the Communist] always accused others of belonging to the petty bourgeoisie. The fact is, he himself has a certain special "ism" of his own. He makes himself different from the ordinary in every respect. As to the comrades under him, he does not care a bit how they are, whether they are sick or not, dead or alive.

Right! crows are black everywhere. Our XX comrade is just this type.

They talk nicely—friendly love, what not. But they have no sympathy man to man. They seem to be all smiles when you meet them. But these smiles are skin deep; they come not from their heart. At the slightest provocation they would blow up; they would assert themselves and tell you off.

The general effect of Wang's essays were similarly harsh and bitter. He called the Marxists "half-baked"; he denied being a "follower of equalitarianism," but said, "To have clothing in three colours and meals in five kinds may not be absolutely necessary or reasonable." For several weeks, a series of "*tou cheng* [or struggle] meetings" were held against him. He disappeared later, and nothing more was heard from him.

But Wang was not the only one singled out for ideological whipping. There were others, among them the famous woman novelist Ting Ling.

On March 9, 1942, Ting Ling published a short essay entitled "Some Thoughts on Women's Day" in the Yenan *Liberation Daily*. It was soon singled out as an attempt to attack "the entire social system of the liberated areas." She was accused of describing the women of Yenan as objects of slander and ridicule to men, of insulting the leaders of Yenan (calling them "dolts"), and painting the entire Yenan area as inferior to Kuomintang territory, or even worse than feudal society. And the Party severely denounced her short story "*In the Hospital*" as an attempt to "slander the entire life of the Party and the liberated areas." Her accusers presented the case as follows:

A Shanghai girl, a Party member who was fond of society and fun, went to Yenan. "She was sure she would be an active political worker." But as "her chief interest was literature, she might have become a great writer." Owing to wartime needs, however, and the fact that she had been trained for a few years as a nurse, she was not made a political worker or a writer but persuaded to join a newly established hospital. According to Ting Ling, "The Party's needs were clamped on her head like an iron ring—how could she disobey orders?" Therefore she expressed indignation on behalf of this girl, considering that the Party had wasted a genius. In her eyes, Yenan was a place where talent was disregarded. Everything there was wrong. There was "desolation all around," and the place "stank." . . .

Naturally the hospital was as backward as the rest of Yenan. Thus the heroine of the story said: "You wonder why the director is no good, but do you know what he used to be? An illiterate dolt! The instructor was just a cowherd brought up by the army—what does he understand? I agree they are all no good and we need a change, but who is there to replace them? I tell you, those above are just the same." She was indignant and pessimistic. "What do these workers and peasants know about leading a revolution? All they can do is work their fingers to the bone—they don't know the first thing about medicine or nursing.[40]

The story's heroine was friendly toward one of the chief doctors, whom Ting Ling described as "a middle-aged man with a gentlemanly air" and "a surgeon who sometimes wrote short stories and plays." The Party also disapproved of Ting Ling's sympathy with this character.

Apparently, however, Ting Ling received better treatment than Wang Shih-wei. She did not immediately disappear; she repented during the struggle meetings, and took great pains to criticize herself. At any rate, her self-criticisms were evidently accepted by the authorities and she remained prominent in the Party until 1957, when the Party opened the old wounds once again in the "Hundred Flowers" campaign, the struggle against "rightists."

In any case, the *Cheng Feng* campaign was quite an event in the Party. Everyone was involved; newspapers, magazines, wall newspapers, and all other possible forms of persuasive communications were mobilized. According to an official communiqué of the Party's Department of Propaganda, the period of ideological study was set at three months for Party organs and two months for all Party schools.[41] Then there was a period for the investigation of Party work, followed by a time in which members in individual organs and schools were to draw conclusions on the standard of their comrades' work. Eighteen documents were assigned as required reading and ideological guides. These included writings by Mao, Kang Sen, Liu Shao-chi, Chen Yun, and Stalin, along with other official documents of the Party.

The principal method of reform was criticism and self-criticism. All members were warned not to "calculatingly protect themselves by keeping silent or avoiding their own mistakes while only attacking others." Self-criticism here meant complete public confession.

Very little information is available on what actually transpired during the *Cheng Feng* movement. While the Party generally takes great pride in and frequently refers to this specific campaign, they rarely reveal the details of its operation. Foes of the regime often describe the entire campaign as a reign of terror in which Communists mercilessly attacked each other; orthodox Communists choose to refer to it as a major ideological and educational reform. In any event, it is clear that a major thought-reform operation was carried out and that the method of criticism and self-criticism was employed extensively with dramatic psychological effect.

But it should also be pointed out that the movement did not appear as a purge in any way similar to the Russian attempt in 1933–35. Very few of the top leadership of the Party were singled out to air their mistakes in public confession. Moreover, the size of the Party membership did not seem to diminish, as was the case in Russia. Very possibly, *Cheng Feng* was intended simply as an ideological and disciplinary measure to combat hostile ideologies and to introduce Mao's doctrines in a serious and formal manner.

The fact that the most celebrated *Cheng Feng* cases happened to concern individuals prominent in the field of art and literature rather than in politics is easy to understand. There is no doubt that on trial during the movement was not merely the "fragile and wicked petty bourgeois mentality" but also the political theories held by such foes of Mao as Li Li-san, Chen Shao-yu (Wang Ming) and Ching Pang-hsien (Po Ku). These were Communists with firm Soviet support at the time, and they could not be openly branded as traitors to the Party or as Trotskyites, and they were attacked indirectly instead. There is every reason to believe that they were the people in Mao's mind when he made his cynical and cutting attacks against formalism, subjectivism, and sectarianism within the Party. His article entitled "In Opposition to Party Formalism" and Liu Shao-chi's "Liquidation of Menshevik Thought" seem to be specially directed against Chen Shao-yu and his clique of "Moscow-returned" students.

There was perhaps another even more important reason behind the ideological remolding campaign of 1942. Mao had not yet achieved his later reputation as a theoretician. He was known as a practical revolutionary who had done as much fighting and organizing as he had theorizing and preaching. And the same was true of his chief supporters—Chou En-lai, Chen Yun, Chen Po-ta and Liu Shao-chi. Judging from their writings and speeches, their belief was that a true revolutionary theoretician was one who had had practical experience in the tasks of the Party; possession of mere bookish knowledge of Marxism-Leninism was not only insufficient, but undesirable and even harmful. Very clearly, Chen Shao-yu did not meet this requirement. Nor did many of the intellectuals in the Party. Their interest in the Chinese Communist revolution was genuine, perhaps; but their determination to obey the leadership of those who were less educated and less sophisticated than themselves was probably questionable. This was particularly true among the artists and writers, who could be so fired by a revolutionary idea as to be willing to sacrifice their lives for the cause, but who were not naturally moved to accept rigid doctrinal discipline.

Irritated by the display of superiority and even arrogance among some of the intellectuals and determined to establish their own political line, Mao and his close associates sought in *Cheng Feng* to ensure that only the standpoint of the proletariat was accepted as the correct one, and to make it clear that the only way to acquire this correct attitude was to "learn from" and "serve the workers, peasants, and soldiers." Those who showed reluctance to conform, such as Wang Shih-wei, became targets of attack and were set up as symbols of the deceitful, designing, and two-faced wickedness of the bourgeoisie.

There is another element to the story, too. Realism was the accepted doctrine that guided the writing and thinking of all Chinese intellectuals at the time. Many writers first attracted the attention and favor of the Chinese Communists because of their realistic portrayal of the unhappy experiences of feudalism and imperialism, and because of their bitter attacks on the corruption and inefficiency of the Nationalist Government. Such realism greatly aided the cause of Chinese Communism, but it obviously could not be tolerated when the writers tried to maintain the same objectivity toward the Party. Moreover, the Party had set a special task requiring the undivided attention of all artists and writers at the time. This was to participate in propaganda-agitation work among the peasants, workers, soldiers, and Chinese people as a whole. In other words, art and literature were required, as a Communist expression puts it, to serve the political purpose of the proletariat. Artists and writers had to abandon their personal goals

and private ivory towers and go to the masses—to engage in propaganda work that was often blatantly undisguised and rarely intel-
lectually sophisticated. They were re-educated to believe that "art
for art's sake" or "literature for literature's sake" was blasphemy.
A composer who had aspired to be a Beethoven or Mozart was
forced to tinker with tunes for worker-agitation songs; a soprano
who had dreamed of being a prima donna found herself conducting illiterate peasants in group singing; a painter who had hoped
to be a Rembrandt was limited to drawing posters and wall newspapers. The shock and agony were particularly great for those
who were already established in their respective fields.

Mao was not, however, totally uninterested in preserving or
cultivating the talents of artists and writers. It was simply that he
did not feel that it was misusing their creative gifts to harness
them to the needs of the Party. This was fundamental to Mao's
doctrine, and the measures he took demonstrate his shrewdness in
shattering the intellectuals' feeling of superiority, suppressing their
individualistic and libertarian tendencies, and thus preparing them
to accept the concept of the "infinite wisdom" of the proletariat
and the "destined leadership" of the Party.

After the dramatic cases of Wang Shih-wei and Ting Ling in the
Cheng Feng of 1942, the Party did not attempt any similar movement on such a scale until 1948, when another famous writer became the target of ideological attack by not only those within the
Party but all others under Communist rule. (One year before the
formal establishment of the Peking regime in 1949, the Communists were already well established in northwest China and on their
way to victory elsewhere.) The victim this time was Hsiao Chun,
who had achieved national fame through his novel, *Rural Villages
in August*, published during the Sino-Japanese War.

Hsiao Chun's original name was Liu Tien-chun. He was a pro-
tegé of Lu Hsun and quite prominent among leftist writers in
China before he went to Yenan in 1940. Needless to say, he was
more than welcome there; but it did not take him long to become
dissatisfied with his comrades. Like Wang Shih-wei and Ting
Ling, he too had a number of unpleasant things to say about the
Party during the *Cheng Feng* of 1942. The *Chieh Fang Jih Pao*

(*Liberation Daily*) carried an article by him on April 8 of that year, entitled "On Comradeship and Forbearance Among Comrades." In it, he remarked:

> In recent years, I have had more contact with revolutionaries. But I feel that the wine of "comradely love" is being increasingly watered down. Although I know the reason, I cannot but feel sad. . . . I do not wish to see, nor let the readers see, the bullets fired by one comrade penetrate the chest of another comrade.

Hsiao Chun was accused later of depicting Yenan as a "dungeon full of devils and monsters."[42] Curiously enough, the Communists did not open fire on him immediately in 1942, but waited until 1948 to "settle their account."[43]

V-J Day came, and Hsiao Chun marched with the Communist troops into Northeast China, where he had been born. He was assigned the job of publishing the *Wen Hua Pao,* or *Culture News,* in Harbin, a publication that first appeared in May, 1946. Apparently with every good intention, but nevertheless overlooking the limits prescribed for Party criticism, Hsiao Chun more than once published ideas that were unpalatable to Party authorities.

He was so pained by the bloody class struggle required by the land reform policy that he called the program an "unprecedented act of piracy":

> The so-called democracy, revolution, communism appear to be contrary to the ordinary moral principles. The idea of dividing up people's land and taking away their property . . . is an unprecedented act of piracy indeed. Even people of such notoriety as Li Tzu-cheng and Chang Hsien-chung dared not use a method of this kind. The Manchus came from a different race and so did the Japanese. Yet neither of them resorted to a method of this kind. Why should the Communists be so unkind and so heartless?[44]

Perhaps what irritated the Party authorities even more was Hsiao Chun's abomination of the Soviet Union. In an article entitled "On Various Shades of Imperialism," published in the fifty-third issue of his journal, he roundly denounced Moscow; the behavior of the Russians in Harbin was especially nauseous to him, and he ridiculed them as "the garbage of the Soviet people." In another article, with the sarcastic title of "Discourteous not to

Return a Courtesy," Hsiao stood in favor of taking some action against the Russians. The article was written in the form of a story which told of a Russian woman resting in her garden and insulting three Chinese youngsters who were curious about her display of luxury. The language used by the woman was so offensive that one of the Chinese youngsters returned the remarks with a stone.

The Party's organized attack against Hsiao Chun began in the fall of 1948 when Sung Chi-ti and Chin Jen, editors of *Sheng Ho Pao* (*Daily Life*) in Harbin, started to denounce the rebel in articles in their paper. Others followed suit. Finally, a joint meeting was held of fifteen mass organizations in Harbin, headed by the Northeast Branch of the All-China Federation of Literature and Art, to prosecute the struggle against Hsiao. It was followed by a resolution of the Northeast Bureau of the Central Committee of the Chinese Communist Party on the "problem of Hsiao Chun," which became the topic of discussion in all areas under Communist control. Almost immediately, all newspapers and magazines dominated by Communists and fellow travelers broke loose with comments and reports denouncing Hsiao. The curtain had risen on another dramatic scene in the *Cheng Feng* drama. The Communists' decision was that Hsiao was suffering severely from three kinds of "poisonous ideas:" (1) extreme individualism; (2) petty bourgeois mentality and class prejudice; and (3) narrow nationalism.

But it soon became apparent that the humiliation of Hsiao Chun was only one objective of the campaign. He was made a symbol of all "harmful" ideas and thoughts that were prevalent at the time. Confession after confession was made at meetings of artists and writers, who declared their sudden awareness of similar thoughts in their own minds, who swore to "strengthen" themselves with the doctrines of Marxism-Leninism and who "demanded" once again the "correct leadership of the Party in art and literature."

The case of Hsiao Chun was the last episode of the ideological reform activities before 1949; it may even be considered the last scene of the *Cheng Feng* movement. It marked, at any rate, the period during which Mao and his fellow revolutionaries were able to consolidate the Party, ideologically as well as organizationally, to establish their version of Marxism-Leninism, to wage a resolute fight against incompatible ideologies, and to experiment with various methods of thought reform.

Now during the period of the Kuomintang-Communist coalition, the Communists also had propaganda-agitation work to do in three distinctively different areas: (1) in Kuomintang-controlled areas; (2) in Communist-controlled areas; and (3) in areas behind or around the points of Japanese occupation.

Under the vengeful and watchful eyes of the Nationalist Government, Communist propaganda work in Kuomintang areas was necessarily secretive and insurrectional. To be sure, Communists were permitted to publish their newspapers and magazines, but to enlarge their political influence, the Communists had to depend upon other channels of communication besides the printed media. Their guiding policy was, of course, that of the much-publicized "united front," and one of their main objectives was "to win over the allies." This was not a cut-and-dried policy, but one of high flexibility and expediency; Party members were repeatedly educated to apply the policy with skill.

Mao, who was careful never to lose sight of his ultimate objective of Communist revolution, was shrewd enough to realize when he had to make conciliatory or compromising moves. He taught his followers:

In leading the masses to struggle against the enemy, Communists should view things by taking into account the whole situation, the majority and the allies who are working together. They should grasp the principle of subordinating the needs of a part to the needs of the whole. If a certain idea seems practicable from a partial view of the situation but is impracticable from the over-all view, we should subordinate the part to the whole. . . . Communists must never separate themselves from the majority of the masses, leave out of consideration the condition of the majority, and lead a small number of progressives to attempt any venturesome advance; they must attend to forging the links which closely connect the progressives with the broad masses. This is taking the majority into account. Wherever there are democratic parties or individual democrats willing to cooperate with us, Communists must adopt the attitude of discussing matters with them and working together with them.[45]

Mao's formula to "broaden and consolidate the united front" was to apply "the tactics of developing the progressive forces, winning over the middle-of-the-road forces, and opposing the die-hard forces."[46] These were, he added, three "inseparable links." By "middle-of-the-road forces," Mao meant "the middle bourgeoisie, the enlightened gentry and the powerful groups in the provinces," "to be won over only as our allies against imperialism."[47] One can see that the severe thought-reform campaigns and other harsh treatment given such groups later, after the honeymoon period of the Peking regime was finished, were indeed the logical development of Mao's theories at this early period.

Mao was also shrewd in his suggestions for dealing with the die-hard group. "We must also adopt the tactics of struggling against its reactionary policy and carry on a resolute fight against it, ideologically, politically, and militarily"[48]:

If ideologically we could advance a correct revolutionary theory and resolutely explode the counter-revolutionary theory of the die-hards; if politically we take timely tactical steps and resolutely attack their anti-Communist, anti-progressive policy; and if we adopt appropriate military measures and resolutely deal blows to their military offensive—then we shall be able to limit the extent to which their reactionary policy is pursued, force them to recognise the position of the progressive forces, develop the progressive forces, win over the middle-of-the-road forces and isolate the die-hards who are still willing to resist Japan and induce them to stay longer in the anti-Japanese united front. The struggle against the die-hards is waged not only as a measure of defence against attacks so that the progressive forces can be protected against losses and can continue to expand, but also as a means to prolong the die-hards' resistance to Japan and their cooperation with us, thereby averting the outbreak of a large-scale civil war.[49]

It was in this tactical frame of mind that Mao proposed the following propaganda program to be "adhered to firmly":

1. Carry out the Testament of Dr. Sun Yat-sen by arousing the people to resist Japan to a man.
2. Carry out the Principle of Nationalism by resolutely resisting Japanese imperialism and securing the thorough liberation of the

Chinese nation externally and the equality of the nationalities internally.

3. Carry out the Principle of Democracy by granting the people absolute freedom to resist Japan and to save their nation, letting them elect their governments at all levels and setting up the revolutionary democratic political power of the Anti-Japanese National United Front.

4. Carry out the Principle of the People's Welfare by abolishing exorbitant taxes and miscellaneous assessment, reducing rents and interest, enforcing the eight-hour working day, developing agriculture, industry and commerce, and improving the living conditions of the people.

5. Carry out Chiang Kai-shek's declaration that "every person, old and young, in the south or in the north, must take up the responsibility of resisting Japan and defending the soil of our country."[50]

One may wonder whether there was anything at all new in Mao's program, which was essentially the realization of Sun Yat-sen's "Three Peoples' Principles" and a common cry for patriotism by Chiang Kai-shek. There was nothing new, nor did Mao intend anything new. One must remember that the Party was careful never to run "too far ahead of the masses." That principle was clearly at work here. Mao explained:

All these things were put forward in the programme announced by the Kuomintang and the Communist Party. But except for resistance to Japan, the Kuomintang cannot at present carry out any of these things; only the Communist Party and the progressive forces can. This is a programme of the utmost simplicity and has become generally known among the people, but many Communists still do not know how to use it as a weapon to mobilise the masses of the people and isolate the die-hards. Now we must always hold to these five items in the programme and disseminate them by means of public notices, manifestoes, leaflets, essays, speeches, statements etc. . . . It is lawful for us to act in accordance with this programme, while it is unlawful for the die-hards to oppose our carrying it out.[51]

Mao concluded with these forceful and shrewd words: "In the stage of the bourgeois-democratic revolution, this programme of the Kuomintang is basically the same as our programme, but the ideology . . . is entirely different. What we should put into practice is only this common programme of the democratic revolution, but decidedly not the ideology of the Kuomintang."[52]

Mao cautioned his followers that "in the Kuomintang areas, our line is to conceal our crack forces, lie long under cover, accumulate our strength and bide our time, and avoid rashness and exposure." The principles of "justifiability, expediency, and restraint" were the operational guide. Mao went so far as to say that "when any of our Party members are forced to join the Kuomintang, let them join it. . . . Our members should infiltrate extensively into the *pao* and *chia* organisations, educational organisations, economic organisations, and military organisations, and they should extensively develop the work for the united front, i.e. the work of making friends in the Kuomintang's Central army and its troops of miscellaneous brands."[53]

We have gone into the operational principles of Communist political action at such length in order to enable the reader to understand the secretive, intricate, and insurrectional nature of the Communist propaganda-agitation work of this time. The Communists were careful not to make open propaganda about Marxism-Leninism—which, they knew well, would antagonize rather than attract the masses—but to advance the doctrine by indirect and subtle means, invoking patriotism, nationalism, liberty, and democracy. In the meantime, every possible opportunity was seized to create or complicate problems for the Kuomintang, to cause and intensify dissatisfaction with the Nationalists among the people, and to discredit the Government. Perhaps fortunately for the Communists, this was not unduly difficult and the abnormal conditions of the Sino-Japanese War made the work even easier.

The area in which the Communists scored perhaps the greatest propaganda victories was in art and literature, in cultural life in general. Marxism-Leninism had arrived in China at a time when China was desperately searching for new ideas for her national salvation. It was introduced to the country by intellectuals who discussed it along with theories of Adam Smith, John Stuart Mill, Tolstoy, Darwin, Rousseau, Montesquieu, Kropotkin, and T. H. Huxley. Among those who embraced Communism wholly or showed sympathy with it was a small group of artists, writers, and intellectuals. Perhaps they were only vaguely familiar with Marxism-Leninism: In the first decades of the twentieth century, the art and literature of China were ideologically chaotic, and those

seeking inspiration from abroad talked excitedly and often point-
lessly about the aestheticism of Oscar Wilde, naturalism of Gustave
Flaubert, symbolism of Maurice Maeterlinck, neoclassicism of
Anatole France, neohumanism of Goethe and Schiller, or neo-
romanticism of Henrik Ibsen; there were many ism's, of which only
one was Marxism.

At any rate, almost from its birth, the Chinese Communist Party
has formed a curiously important relationship with artists and
writers. Exactly when the Party started to act on Stalin's dictum
that "literature should belong to the Party" cannot easily be ascertained. It can only be said that even in the early 1920's, the Party
vigorously sought alliances with whomever they could among
artists and writers, especially among the newly rising self-styled
leftists and liberals who were frustrated by China's problems and
who, being human, were delighted to get sympathetic attention
from almost anyone.

In 1930, the "Federation of Leftist Writers" was organized.
Communist historians today take pride in pointing out that the
group was organized with the leadership of Communist underground workers in Shanghai. The group had the support and enjoyed the prestige of such great literary figures as Lu Hsun and
Mao Tun.

By this time there had already been clashes between so-called
"revolutionary literature," as represented by the Federation, and
so-called "bourgeois literature." And the debate over the political
function of literature was growing in intensity and scope. At any
rate, it became quite fashionable for writers to promote the cause
of the proletariat, although it would have been more than frowned
at to do so in political circles at that time.

It would be wrong to assume that Communist activities among
artists and writers were tolerated by the Nationalists. It is perhaps closer to the mark to say that the Nationalists were not sufficiently aware of the political usefulness of art and literature either
to be cautious or to take similar actions seriously themselves. It
was quite late by the time the Nationalists realized what they had
overlooked.

Shortly after the outbreak of the Sino-Japanese War, the Federation of Leftist Writers was officially dissolved, apparently with

pressure from the Kuomintang. But the Kuomintang-Comn
coalition in fact made Communist activity in art and literatu.
easier. As a result, the Communists were able later to have remarkable success in their manipulation of artists and writers for
their persuasive communications.

ORGANIZATIONAL AND
OPERATIONAL PATTERN

In order to carry out its gigantic task of mass persuasion, the Chinese Communist Party has at its disposal a machine that controls almost every means of human expression and virtually all the avenues to the Chinese mind. The motor of this immense machine is the *Hsien Chuan Pu,* or Department of Propaganda of the Chinese Communist Party. It is directly under the direction and supervision of the Chairman of the Central Committee of the Party, the Central Political Bureau, and the Central Secretariat.

The Department operates through three major channels. One consists of the propaganda departments or committees maintained in every Party organization at all levels—central, regional, provincial, and local. The second consists of political departments in the armed forces and government agencies in charge of information, publishing, broadcasting, movie production, and various forms of art and literature. The third is formed by numerous "mass organizations" such as the New Democratic Youth Corps, All-China Federation of Writers and Artists, Sino-Soviet Friendship Association, the Democratic Women's Federation, etc.

Coordination of the three channels is achieved by the Party's system of interlocking directorates, in which a few Communist leaders at any level in the Communist organizational structure hold concurrent key positions in the Party, the government, the armed forces, and the "mass organizations." For instance, the secretary of the Party branch (cell) of a commune may also be chairman of the Party's propaganda committee, director of the Department of Culture and Education of the local government, principal of a "Red and Expert School," chairman of the local Sino-Soviet

Friendship Association, and member of a number of local mass organizations.

The Department of Propaganda

The Department of Propaganda was created under the provision of Article 34 of the Constitution of the Party, which states:

> The Central Committee shall, according to the needs of its work, set up departments [such as Organization Department, Propaganda Department, etc.], commissions [such as Military Affairs Commission, Party Press Commission, etc.], and other organs to function in their respective fields under the direction and supervision of the Central Political Bureau of the Central Secretariat, and the Chairman of the Central Committee.

Only meagre information is available about its organization and function, and it seems to be the policy of the Party not to publicize the inside story of how it actually works. However, even a casual reader of Chinese Communist newspapers cannot fail to become aware of the overwhelming power and authority of the Party's propaganda apparatus. The long arm of the Department of Propaganda reaches to a wide variety of activities, ranging all the way from an interpretation of Marxism-Leninism to dealing with simple questions from a peasant in a commune.

Like the Party, which operates on various levels according to the system of "democratic centralism," the propaganda machine has an elaborate hierarchical structure within which several major strata can be distinguished. (Actually, there is a department or committee of propaganda in every Party organization at every level. This is provided by Article 28 of the Constitution which states: "In order to carry on various kinds of practical work, a Party committee at any level may, under its unified leadership, set up departments or commissions to take charge of Party affairs, propaganda and education, military affairs, economic affairs, and the mass work as the situation may require.") At the very top is the Department of Propaganda, directly under the Central Political Bureau. Orders or directives from this central organization are received by propaganda departments of the central bureaus and sub-bureaus, each of which controls several provinces or border regions. Under these are the propaganda departments of the provincial or border regional Party organizations, which, in turn, direct the propaganda departments in cities, counties (*hsien*), and districts (*ch'ü*). At the very bottom stand the propaganda committees of the Party branches (cells), headed by either the secretary of the branch or a Party member chosen for his efficiency in propaganda and organization.

While a department of propaganda at any level directs and supervises all work of persuasion under its jurisdiction, it does not handle all the actual propaganda work. It is not like an information or press service, nor like a propaganda department under Nazi Germany. It is clear Communist doctrine that *every* Communist is a propagandist and that propaganda work must be carried on in all places and at all times:

> What is a propagandist? Not only is the teacher a propagandist, the newspaper reporter a propagandist, the literary writer a propagandist, but all our cadres in all kinds of work are also propagandists. Take, for instance, the military commanders. They do not necessarily issue statements, but when they want to talk to soldiers and deal with people, what are they doing but carrying on propaganda work? Anyone engaged in talking with another person is engaged in propaganda work.[1]

Now consider the duties of a Party branch as specified by the Constitution of the Party:

> 1. To carry on propaganda and organizational work among the masses of the people in order to realize the standpoint advocated by the Party and the decisions of the higher Party organizations;
>
> 2. to pay constant attention to the sentiments and demands of the masses of the people, to report such sentiments and demands to the higher Party organizations, to pay heed to the political, economic and cultural life of the people, and to organize the masses of the people to solve their own problems;
>
> 3. to recruit new members, to collect Party membership dues, to check and verify the records of Party members, and to enforce Party discipline among members; and
>
> 4. to educate the Party members and organize their studies.

With the exception of Item 3, which deals with the management of Party affairs, the listed duties are propaganda activities. The first is clearly propaganda *per se*. The second requires members to report the people's opinions and reactions to higher Party organizations, which undoubtedly need this knowledge of the "psychological climate" for further propaganda activities and plans. The last deals with intra-Party education, and actually aims to equip the Party members with better knowledge, techniques, and methods for mass persuasion work among the masses of people. Since Party branches exist in almost all factories, mines, villages, enterprises, streets, companies of the Army, offices, communes, or schools, "where there are three or more Party members," it is easy to understand how propaganda plans designed by the Department in Peking can be carried to virtually every corner of the nation.

So far as mass persuasion is concerned, the Party branches are the most important units, because they are in the vanguard of the battle to change the minds of men. As Liu Shao-chi puts it, "One of the fundamental organizational principles of the Party is the building of basic organizations and fortresses of the Party on the basis of production units or concentration points of the masses."[2] Not only do they bring the Party closer to the people but they also place it in an advantageous position for propaganda and agitation for higher production. The propagandists of a Party branch in a factory, for instance, are themselves workers. They are supposed to know their fellow workers, their families, backgrounds, tastes, needs, problems, etc., and they know how to talk to them and convince them in their own language.

The Party cells employ various ways and means to bring the Party messages to the people and to urge the people to achieve the Party aims. They publish "wall newspapers" or "blackboard newspapers," produce *tatzepao* (posters), manage collective radio listening posts, distribute pamphlets, present talent shows, organize demonstration parades or accusation meetings, conduct *hsueh hsi,* or study, classes, lead in all kinds of drives or movements, visit families of workers, or simply "talk" to the workers or people in their own surroundings.

One favorite method is to transform themselves and other "aggressive elements" into "model workers," by producing more than is required in the regular schedule, working longer hours, demanding less pay, and "voluntarily contributing" their earnings or energy to whatever cause is being advocated by the Party at the moment. These planted paragons of Communist virtue provide the Party with a constant supply of Stakhanovites, and enable it to "take pride" in the many "wonders" of production and national reconstruction "volunteered" by the people. Such "wonders"—often used by Party authorities as pace-setters—should indeed be credited chiefly to the constant propaganda and persuasion work of the propaganda departments or committees of the Party branches.

It is important to note that the propaganda departments or committees on the lowest levels are important only for their operational activities. They have no part in the general planning of propaganda or agitation policy, which is completely in the hands of the central Department of Propaganda. Their activities follow strictly the pattern and schedule laid down by the national authorities. No local Party branch, for instance, is supposed to decide on any slogans for special occasions, and all are required to use those authorized by the Propaganda Department in Peking. Even unintentional mistakes committed through misunderstanding or misjudgment by lower Party organs are severely reprimanded. The following comments, which appear in *Hsueh Hsi*, illustrate how a Party committee in a small city is severely "criticized" for its failure to follow closely the slogans issued for national use:

In the June 22 issue of the *Tung Pei Jih Pao*, the Northeast Bureau of the Chinese Communist Party published the "Circular of the Heilungkiang Provincial Committee of the Chinese Communist Party Concerning Unauthorized Changes of the Political Slogans for May 1 by the Members of the K'e Shan *hsien* Committee of the Party." According to the circular, the K'e Shan *hsien* committee members made many changes of the political slogans for "May 1" issued by the People's Political Consultative Council and used instead slogans as: to support the Declaration of the Peace Appeal, we should accelerate our Manure and Fertilizer Movement; we should pick up more manure, build more huts, make more hen houses and pig pens . . . and other phrases or sentences which lacked political content. Their reasons for changing the authorized slogans are: the slogans prepared by the PPCC are just general principles; slogans must be united with the actual condition of local areas. At the solemn demonstration meeting, thousands of people of the Ming Li Village of this *hsien*, from the *ch'ü* and village cadres to the masses, never shouted a political slogan. They all shouted: "Pick up manure," "Make pig pen," "Clean hen houses," etc. . . . .

It is necessary, of course, to unite the general political slogans of a national character with actual conditions. It is also necessary to mobilize the masses to support these slogans with actual works. But the correct method of uniting realities is not to change freely or omit political slogans but to use these slogans to educate the masses, to enable them to understand deeply the meaning of every slogan and its close relation to the life of the people of different walks . . . and to elevate the political consciousness of the masses to a higher level.[3]

The local Party branches are also told what priority to give to what issues at what time and to what extent. The only autonomy they have lies in the choice of methods and approaches used to carry out directives from the higher Party organizations.

The Department of Propaganda at Peking guides, directs, and supervises almost all activities of persuasion and indoctrination in the nation. Strictly speaking, it is not an operational organization. It does not actually own or run the Party newspapers, for instance, which are under the jurisdiction of the Party Press Commission (also set up by the Central Committee). It does not operate the radio station, or make motion pictures, since these activities are directed by other government agencies. Nor does it issue orders directly to political commissars and "cultural workers' corps," who are supposed to carry on propaganda and education in the armed forces. It does decide on the content of books and materials for the political *hsueh hsi*, or study, of Party members and the masses and, in fact, edits the majority of such books, but it does not publish them under its own name; such books are published by the companies that are either owned or controlled by the government's Publications Administration. As a matter of fact, most propaganda directives, with the exception of slogans for special occasions, are issued under the name of the propaganda departments of the Party's central bureaus in different administrative areas.

The Department of Propaganda thus prefers to remain in the background, supervising and controlling, and tends to shy away from unnecessary publicity of its own activities. It is one of the most important agencies of the Politburo, yet is comparatively obscure to the public eye. Unlike Dr. Goebbels, who was practically Mr. Nazi Propaganda himself, Lu Ting-i, director of the department, does not personify propaganda in Red China. He does not make frequent public appearances and he is far less known to the Chinese people than Goebbels was to the German public. He does, however, make important pronouncements on certain significant occasions, and he is frequently and widely quoted by journalists and propaganda cadres, if not by the masses.

The propaganda units of the Party's central bureaus and sub-bureaus in the various geographical regions prepare periodical "propaganda outlines" (*hsien chuan ta kang*) or "important points on propaganda" for "propagandists" and "party reporters" at local levels. In some cases, these outlines are circulated every month; in others, less frequently. Special outlines are distributed when there are special issues. These outlines cover a wide variety of topics and instruct local propagandists on exactly how they should express themselves on a given issue.

In addition to the "propaganda outlines," the propaganda departments of the bureaus and sub-bureaus put out "propaganda handbooks" (*hsien chuan shou tz'e*), published by the official People's Publishing Company, which has branches all over the Chinese mainland. Among such handbooks are the *Current Affairs Handbook*, published in Peking, the *Propagandists' Handbook* in Sian, the *Propagandist* in Hankow, and the *Canton Propagandists* in Canton. All these are small booklets somewhat smaller than an American pocket paperback book. In each issue there are articles on special occasions and instructions to propagandists as to what they should stress in their speeches to the masses; articles interpreting current affairs; questions and answers on problems likely to be raised by the common people; reference materials for "wall newspapers" or "blackboard newspapers"; songs that can be used in mass meetings; cartoons which could be reproduced by local talent without much difficulty; and discussions on propaganda methods and appeals.

Consider, for instance, the November 25, 1951, issue of the *Canton Propagandists* (*Kuang Chou Hsian Chuan Yuan*). In this

45-page biweekly, there are articles, stories, statistics, cartoons, and many other materials prepared to help propagandists to advance such major programs advocated by the regime as the Increase Production and Practice Austerity Movement, the Resist-America Aid-Korea Campaign, the Marriage Law, Patriotic Pact, Suppression of Counterrevolutionaries, etc. This issue was published at the time when the Production-Increase and Austerity Movement was in full swing, and one-third of it dealt with this special campaign—a response to a call made by Mao Tse-tung in the third session of the National Congress of the People's Political Consultative Council, which ended in November, 1951. The first article, "How to Develop the Large-Scale Production-Increase and Austerity Movement in Canton," explains the meaning and objectives of the movement and specifies methods of conducting "ideological mobilization" for it. The second piece recommends learning the working method of Ho Chien-hsiu, a much-publicized woman model worker. This article is followed by two cartoons, and the third article deals with the "plans" of a group of workers of Locomotive No. 562 of the Canton Railroad Sub-bureau to increase production by hard work and thrift. Then follows a column of statistical information showing how much one can waste through ignorance of thrift and correct working methods. A seven-page article, "Questions and Answers on the Korean Situation," is specially provided as "reference material for propagandists in their talks." Most of the questions are similar to the following, considered likely to be raised by the common people: "What is the recent development of the Korean situation?" "What is our attitude in the Korean peace talks?" "What is the fundamental spirit of our proposals in the peace parleys?" "Why and how does America obstruct and delay these negotiations?" The issue also contains a "folk song" called "Blessings of Peace-loving people," written in popular story-telling rhythmic form and local Canton dialect. Another article, entitled "To propagandize the Marriage Law under Banners and Drums," suggests to propagandists what to do and say in explaining the law to the people. For the propaganda of the suppression of "counterrevolutionaries," there is a piece telling how a factory worker successfully cooperated with fellow workers and "eliminated" Liang Lin, "a secret agent and remaining element of feudalism." Needless to say, such "model experience" is to be studied and followed.

Such propaganda handbooks served as an important link between Peking and the masses—particularly during the early years of the Chinese Communist regime, when a nationwide propaganda system or organization was yet to be developed—by means of the "propagandists" who used them in the "propaganda networks" (an activity of the Party to be discussed below). They began gradually to disappear after 1954 and 1955, when their function was apparently taken over by Party newspapers, both central and regional; special magazines for indoctrination purposes, such as *China Youth* for the All-China Democratic Youth Corps and *Hsueh Hsi* (*Study*) and later *Hung Chi* (*Red Flag*); and instructions offered to local propagandists over radio stations.

The Propaganda Networks

Until 1951, the Party lacked a permanent, well-planned machinery and program to carry out nationwide propaganda activities. The various campaigns and movements—such as those for signatures to the Stockholm Peace Appeal, for the glorification of "model workers," etc.—as many Communist newspapers freely admit, were temporary movements, suddenly popping up and quickly dying out, creating only a temporary fever of enthusiasm among the Party rank and file and among the people.

In January, 1951, obviously trying to "tighten its unity with the masses," the Party launched the gigantic project of setting up a permanent propaganda system that would radiate into the masses and guide them along the line of orthodox policy. This project was the "nationwide propaganda networks." Their establishment opened a new era in the history of Communist propaganda in China; it enabled the Party to spread new propaganda personnel over the whole country and to advance from theoretical to more practical goals.

On January 1, 1951, the Central Committee of the Party issued an official order: "Decisions on the Establishment of Propaganda Networks for the Whole Party among the Masses of the People."[4] This basic document was presented for study to all Party branches in the country and was followed by a flurry of reports and criticisms in newspapers and magazines, and by group discussions. The first paragraph described the necessity and urgency for more propaganda work among the people. Remarking that propaganda had fallen off in many parts of the country or had ceased completely, it charged that many Party organizations at various levels had overlooked the importance of carrying on propaganda on a permanent basis. The result, according to the document, was the rise of reactionary propaganda and harmful rumors now constantly heard among the people. Further, the document criticized Party members for excessive use of administrative commands in their work and for failure to deal with the masses through the methods of persuasion and explanation. In order to rectify such errors, the Party had decided to install "propagandists" in every Party branch and "reporters" to direct Party organs at various levels, and thus to establish a definite nationwide propaganda network.

Under the new arrangement, a "propagandist" was not just a regular worker in the Party's Propaganda Department or the Army's propaganda troupe—who put up posters, prepared wall newspapers, gave street-corner shows, or shouted slogans at mass meetings. A "propagandist" of a "network" was supposed to be constantly carrying on, by simple popular means, propaganda and agitation among the people in his environment. He was supposed to:

1. use simple and popular forms to propagate among and explain to the people in his area current national and international affairs, policies of the Party and government, the people's tasks (especially the most direct and urgent tasks of those whom he is addressing), and "model experiences" of the masses of people in production and other works;

2. refute current reactionary rumors and erroneous ideas among the people;

3. stimulate or agitate people to obtain "model experience" in order to accomplish their tasks in an aggressive manner; and

4. report regularly the conditions among the people to higher Party officials, so that they may decide on adequate propaganda content and methods at different times.

Propagandists are chosen from among members of the Party

and the New Democratic Youth Corps (and those model workers or revolutionary activists who volunteer to serve under the guidance of the Party). Party branch secretaries and committee members are also expected to work in this capacity, as are those officials who are in constant contact with the masses of the people: cadres in unions, cooperatives, districts (*ch'ü*, a subdivision of a county), or villages; school teachers; staff members of mass education centers; and editors of wall newspapers. All appointments of propagandists must be passed on by the propaganda committees of the Party branches and also approved by a higher Party organ. The selection of propaganda material is made by the Party branches.

All propagandists are under the direct supervision of the Party branches. It is repeatedly emphasized in official directives that the success of propaganda depends on the assistance and guidance of Party branches. For instance, in North China and Central-South China, all Party members and cadres in factories, schools, mines, and government agencies are instructed to assist the Party branches in directing the propagandists' work. For this purpose, the Party branches issue working directives, prepare propaganda materials, call meetings of propagandists, and plan, review, and criticize their work.[6]

A propagandist's daily tasks are not, however, specifically prescribed by Party authorities; they vary from place to place and time to time. But the main principle, to be followed by all propagandists, is that their activities must always be closely related to the tasks of the people who form their audience. The main forms or types of propaganda include: interviewing, passing on of information, newspaper reading groups, listening to broadcasts and rebroadcasting to the people, preparing propaganda posters or other materials, and editing wall newspapers. All propagandists are encouraged to find their own methods, so long as they will achieve the goals prescribed by the Party. In a book entitled *How to be a Propagandist*, edited and published by the People's Publishing Company, more than fifty propagandists tell of their experiences and recommend the methods with which they have experimented successfully. For instance, a 51-year-old propagandist, an old-timer in a railroad factory at Dairen, suggests the use of daily conversation for propaganda purposes. He relates that when he was first asked to be a propagandist, he often called meetings and addressed the people, informing them of what he had learned from the Party. But he soon sensed the people's indifference and noticed a drop in attendance. Then he changed his method: He began to plant propaganda in his daily conversation with co-workers, and found this most successful:

One Foot in the Puddle[5]

It was early dawn after rain and still dark. Workers on their way to the factory were walking on a narrow street. Without paying too much attention, one worker stepped with one foot into a puddle of muddy water. He was very angry after he pulled his foot out of the mud.

I [the propagandist] hurried to him and asked: 'What happened?'

'Damn it! I fell in the puddle!' he replied with anger.

'I just had a fall, too, and I surely cursed well!'

'Whom did you curse?'

'I cursed the American devils.'

'Why do you curse the American devils for your fall?'

'If the American devils had not invaded us and bombed our Northeast, would we have to have protection from air raids and always be in a black-out? We would have our street lights lit until morning and then we wouldn't fall or step into puddles. Whom do you think I should curse besides those damn American devils?'

I immediately added: 'If I could curse them to death, I would surely curse them all day long in my home. But cursing alone won't help. This means that we should put more effort into production.'

At this point, the muddy factory worker said: 'You're right.'

Other stories of this kind, of how propagandists used different methods in carrying out their agitation work, practically flooded the Communist newspapers during the first months after the propaganda networks were inaugurated.

As an illustration of a typical pattern of operation, the following "propaganda plan," prepared and put into practice jointly by two propagandists for a one-month period, is fairly representative of the work done in small villages, factories, and farms. The two operatives were T'su Ch'ang-cheng and T'su Pi-ch'eng, of a small village in North Kiangsu. Their plans, apparently approved by

Party authorities, were given considerable publicity—being pub-
lished in the Shanghai *Liberation Daily* (May 7, 1951) and in the
Current Affairs Handbook (No. 19, July 20, 1951), published in
Peking:

A. *Objectives and Requirements of Propaganda:*

1. There are 16 families in the section. Each of us will take care
   of 8 families. We both guarantee that every member of the
   16 families will receive constantly the education of the Resist-America Aid-Korea Movement. At the end of half a
   month, we will compare notes to see which one of us is doing a better job of propaganda.

2. In addition to the fixed objects of propaganda (the 16 families), we will talk to anyone whom we meet. The motto is
   not to waste one single minute or ignore one single individual.
   We should change the "conversation on personal affairs" into
   a "conversation on current affairs" and thus develop the
   habit of carrying on propaganda at all times and places.

3. The general task of the propaganda in the Resist-America
   Aid-Korea campaign should be united with the propaganda
   of the actual tasks carried on in the community. In the patriotic movement of increasing production, we will not only set
   up our own plans of production but will also mobilize all the
   people in the community to do the same. We will aim at
   mobilizing people to plant 40 acres of cotton and 60 trees
   and to invest in 30 shares of the local co-op; persuading
   55 people to sign the Peace Appeal (Stockholm) and vote
   in the movement for solving the problem of Japan by a
   united effort (as opposed to the Peace Treaty signed with
   Japan by the United States and most of the other belliger-
   ents at San Francisco); organizing 30 people to participate
   in the demonstration parade in celebration of May 1; and
   directing the masses to do a good job in suppressing the
   counterrevolutionaries.

B. *Content of Propaganda:*

1. To make everyone in the community understand that to oppose America and aid Korea is the only way to protect his
   home and defend the country; that the actual task of the
   Resist-America Aid-Korea Movement is to increase production and do a good job in one's own field; that the Chinese

and Korean armies will definitely win the war, and that the American devils will eventually be defeated. Meanwhile we should point out the possible difficulties that may be encountered, explain the experiences in China's War of Liberation, and enable the masses to understand correctly the victorious situation at present and not to be disturbed by temporary setbacks.

2. To propagate the ten principles in the speed-up movement in production and organize the masses of the people to participate in the movement through these principles.

3. To propagate current information on the suppression of counterrevolutionaries on the basis of the "Law on the Punishment of Counterrevolutionaries" recently made public by the government.

4. To propagate the advantages of a close relation between co-ops and the people and thus encourage people to purchase shares.

5. To propagate the meaning of signing the World Peace Appeal and voting on the Japanese question, and to explain the reasons for participating in the demonstration parade on May 1.

C. *Source of Material for Propaganda:*

1. To attend the meetings for propagandists punctually, listen carefully to the lectures, and study the propaganda materials.

2. To read newspapers, propaganda handbooks, and any other material handed down from the higher Party organization and to keep constantly in touch with the secretary of the Party branch.

3. To gather reactions from the masses.

4. To maintain constant contact with the *ch'ü* committee of the Party through letters and in person.

D. *Forms and Methods of Propaganda:*

1. To organize four group discussions during this month. At least one of them should be a discussion meeting of women.

2. To conduct individual propaganda or informal conversation at least twice a day and make it a habit to do so.

3. To organize a newspaper-reading group, and read the *Ta Chung Pao* [*The Daily of the Masses*, published in North Kiangsu] every three days. We will take turns in reading newspapers.

4. To put out a "propaganda bulletin board" on current affairs and local news. The board is to be supplied with new material every three days.
5. To grasp every opportunity for propaganda such as working, walking, etc.
6. To make use of the aggressive activists in the masses. It is our plan to make use of Tsu Chang-yu [name of a child] to carry on propaganda among the eighteen children in the community. We are planning to educate and use Siao Chi-yuan [name of a woman] to carry on propaganda among the twelve women in the section.

How successful such propagandists are in winning the people to the cause of the Party cannot be easily ascertained. However, one thing is certain: It did not take the Chinese Communist Party long to establish its "propaganda network" over almost the entire country. According to figures released by the Party in December, 1951, there were more than 1,550,000 propagandists in the whole country by October, 1951.[7] The average percentage of propagandists in each factory, farm, or production unit was about 10 per cent of the total. In the Northeast alone, there were 117,823 propagandists in 1950; it was the plan of the area Party authorities to increase the number to 200,000 in 1951.[8] In an electric power plant at Dairen, the number of propagandists was 10 per cent of the total work force; in a mine at Anshan, 6 per cent; in another chemical plant at Mukden, 13 per cent.[9] Within two years, there was hardly any place in China where a person could be free from the persistent persuasion of these propagandists.

The introduction of the propaganda networks changed considerably the social life of peasants, factory workers, and other people on lower social levels. Perhaps never before in their lives had these people been so constantly persuaded to do so many things, attend so many meetings, sign so many pacts—and do so "voluntarily." According to one official report, in two weeks the Party secretary of the City Committee of Peng Chi made 18 reports; the high-ranking cadres in factories and mines made 625 reports to a total audience of 70,000; there were 270 group discussions in which 25,000 people participated; 30 accusation meetings and 15 oral contests were held. In addition, there were evening story-telling meetings, memory meetings (where participants were expected to "recall" sufferings in the "old, feudalistic" days), and farewell meetings to the people joining the armed forces. Then, cadres were organized to conduct interviews in every family in the city.[10] From July 10 to July 20, 1951, in Chaoan, a *hsien* in Kwangtung, there were 8,085 grievance and accusation meetings, including 1,347 mass meetings and 6,738 ones for small groups. Every inhabitant attended an average of at least three such meetings.[11]

The content of material used by propagandists in the early years of the Peking regime was summarized in the following statement made by the Department of Propaganda of the Party's Northeast Bureau:

Content of mass propaganda varies with the tasks or responsibilities prescribed by the Party at special times and with the different stages of historical development. At present, our mass propaganda efforts are mainly as follows: to develop continuously the Resist-America Aid-Korea Protect-Home Defend-Nation Movement; to elevate the consciousness of the masses of people in anti-imperialism, patriotism and internationalism, to hate, condemn and despise American imperialism and eliminate all the poisonous elements of befriending America, respecting America and fearing America [that are] spread by the running dogs of American imperialists; to ascertain the self-confidence and self-respect of the masses in their love for the fatherland and people; and to develop further the aggressiveness and creativeness of the masses of people in high-speed labor production in order to increase constantly the production rate for the consolidation of national defense, development of the national economy, and struggle for the defense of world peace.[12]

The order to establish propaganda networks stipulated that the Party propagandists should meet at least once a month—at most, once a week—to discuss their instructions and the work accomplished. The *hsien*, or county, Party organ was to convene a monthly meeting of propagandists and their representatives. On behalf of the Party's *hsien* committees, the district (*ch'ü*) committees were required constantly to direct the propaganda of the Party branches and to decide on the scope, aims, and methods to be used by each, according to its own conditions. In rural areas, where transportation conditions were poor, district committees followed a system of setting up "instruction relay posts." Selected propagandists representing branch propaganda departments were summoned to receive instructions with regard to propaganda content, methods, and approaches.

These "instruction relay posts" soon spread all over the country. As early as 1951, the Department of Propaganda in the province of Hopei reported that, according to incomplete statistics, there were 710 posts in 29 *hsien*. Besides passing on instructions to Party branches, they also served to educate and train propagandists. In Hopei Province, the heads of all such posts were members of the *ch'ü* committees charged with educational responsibilities. And there, and elsewhere, they not only gave instructions on propaganda to Party branches, but also supervised the "political study" of Party members at a lower level and in turn reported their progress to their superiors.[13]

Realizing that members of Party branches as well as of the *ch'ü* committees were often of low cultural levels, the Central Committee decided that propagandists alone would not be enough to enable the masses to understand fully the Party's policies, especially those designed for special occasions. The Party believed that the directing personnel of the Party's organs at other levels should be available to make systematic reports or lectures on current affairs, policies, tasks, and experiences. For this purpose, "reporters" or "reporting personnel" were installed in Party committees in every province, city, administrative district, *hsien*, or *ch'ü*.

Reporters, as regulated by the Party's Central Committee, "are propagandists of a higher rank and therefore are directing personnel of propagandists.[14] Forming the large army of reporters were secretaries and responsible members of Party committees at all levels, from the *ch'ü* to the province, and Party members holding responsible positions in government agencies. Every "reporter" is required to make a political report at least once every two months before a large gathering of representatives of the masses of people (the workers and peasants). Subject and content must be approved in advance by the secretary of the Party committee to which the reporter belongs. After delivering a speech or completing a speaking tour, the reporter is expected to submit to the secretary of his committee a report both about his talks and about the reactions of the audience; the secretary is responsible for going through these reports and offering any assistance or guidance necessary to guarantee that the reporters' work is always of the approved kind. They are also encouraged to recommend good reports for publication in newspapers.

There is unquestionably a spark of genius in the Party's use of "reporters" and "propagandists." Since most of the propagandists are ordinary Party members, whose words might not be accepted as authoritative, their work, as the Party recognizes, must be reinforced by Party leaders, who are more likely to command the respect of the common people. This function is served by the reporters. On the other hand, since the propagandists work among the people day in and day out, they are expected to create a climate that will make it easier for the reporters to consummate the conquest of people's minds. Furthermore, since both reporters and propagandists are supervised by the Party committees, the Department of Propaganda of the Central Committee is, on paper at least, in a good position to control and direct all propaganda activities.

A word on the principles generally followed by the Party in this field may be useful here. The first principle is that in setting up a propaganda network in any area, all members of the Party committee in the area, especially the Party secretary, must be thoroughly indoctrinated as to the significance of the project before they are presented with definite plans and instructions for carrying it out. The Communist press and propagandists' handbooks frequently repeat that propaganda networks can be established successfully only where the members of the local committee are convinced of its urgency and importance. This is an important point because all responsible leaders of the Party committees are authorized to appoint propagandists, as well as reporters. The Party has admitted that in many areas its leaders are indifferent and simply fill the quota of propagandists set by their superiors, and that in other areas, they simply pass the job on to unions, mass education centers, youth corps, or even entertainment places. The Party cannot afford to allow this laxity because its aim is a centralized control of all propaganda activities, conducted on a permanent basis.

A second principle followed in setting up propaganda networks is that they should be closely connected with production and with the political movements of the people. There are two reasons why propaganda work should be closely associated with production: First, the Party wants to follow the policy that "we do what we propagate," thus making propaganda more timely and stimulating; secondly, it is among producers that the Party can best find "activists" to train for propaganda work. For, according to the Party, "activists" discovered through mass movements are often effective propagandists, once they have received adequate training and indoctrination. "Activists" who are themselves workers know the people in their own labor groups and are familiar with their sentiments and conditions; they can talk the people's language and are accepted more readily than outsiders would be. It is for this same reason that Party branches are given direct supervision over their propagandists.

In the January 1, 1952, issue of *Jen Min Jih Pao*, there appeared an article entitled "The Condition of the Party's Propaganda Networks after One Year of Development, and Objectives of Further Consolidation and Development in the Future." This 2,000-word article reviewed the accomplishments and failures of this gigantic project since it was inaugurated in January, 1950, and it reveals clearly the strength of the huge army of propagandists and reporters in modern Communist China.

According to this article, there were, in December, 1950, already more than 1,920,000 propagandists in the country. The estimated figures for the number of propagandists in each of the six regional administrative areas were as follows:

North China	606,000
Northeast	300,000
East	650,000
Central-South	236,000
Southwest	85,000
Northwest	30,000

Of the provinces, Hopei and Shantung had the largest number of propagandists, each with more than 330,000. In both Hopei and Chahar, the number of propagandists was more than 1 per cent of the total population. In Shantung and Shansi, the number was also close to 1 per cent.

It was the plan of the Party to increase the number of propagandists to 4 or 5 million by the end of 1952:

> In addition to consolidating the present system of propaganda networks, we should aim in the future at further developing our army of propagandists. . . . Firstly, our national development of propaganda networks is still not sufficiently extensive. In many areas today, no propagandist is yet installed; in other areas where propagandists exist, the development is far from being sufficient. Secondly, to judge by the scope of the Party's propaganda work and the task to be taken care of in the future, the number of our existing propagandists is comparatively small and far from satisfying our demand. China is a big country of more than 500,000,000 population and the set-up of the Party's propaganda machinery must necessarily be an unusually enormous one. In order to have our propaganda work constantly penetrated to the broad masses, we must have an army of organized propagandists, much larger than the size we have today. Therefore, we cannot be satisfied with the present force of our propagandists but must continuously do our utmost to further recruit and organize propagandists. We have now more than 5,800,000 members of the Party and 5,500,000 members of the New Democratic Youth Corps. In addition, we have a large number of revolutionary activists among the masses. Thus it is completely possible to systematically develop our army of propagandists. By the end of 1952, we should work for the completion of the installing of propagandists in all Party branches. . . . Our goal is to have 4,000,000 to 5,000,000 propagandists who will form the foundation on which further consolidated development is to be made.[15]

Significantly, not much has been said about the propaganda networks since 1953, although occasional books are published on the subject. A few interviews conducted by this author with Chinese refugees in Hong Kong in 1960 led him to believe that the system as it was designed in 1950 continued to operate, but that more and more, propaganda activities became the regular tasks of various units of the Party, government, and mass organizations.

5. MASS COMMUNICATION: THE SYSTEM

A French correspondent who visited Red China in 1956 reported:

> The head of a good Chinese citizen today functions like a sort of radio receiving set. Somewhere in Peiping buzzes the great transmitting station which broadcasts the right thought and the words to be repeated. Millions of heads faithfully pick them up, and millions of mouths repeat them like loud-speakers.[1]

This must sound hard to believe. For Communist China, in spite of its ambitious program of modernization, continues to be handicapped by a high illiteracy rate and inadequate communication facilities. Although newspaper circulation, for instance, jumped from 3.4 million in 1951 to 15 million in 1958, and magazine circulation from 900,000 to 17 million in the same period,[2] and even if we doubled these figures, they would still trail far behind those for the United States,* a country with a far smaller population.

In a country like the United States, where the people are daily bombarded with messages from the mass media, it is understandable how and why the entire nation can become acquainted with a new product, a new catch phrase, or a new jingle in a relatively short time. It is not at all uncommon to see a first-grader humming a song on the "hit parade" or even dancing to the tune of a beer commercial. But imagine the task of even the most powerful Madison Avenue manipulators if they were asked to introduce a few political concepts into China without the benefit of the mass media that are at their command here. And imagine further the complexity of the problem if the concepts should deal with ab-

* The newspaper circulation in the United States is around 56 million.

stract entities that are alien to the audience, such as "class consciousness," "democratic dictatorship," or "system of exploitation."

Yet this is exactly what has been attempted in Communist China. In 1951, only two years after the Peking regime was established, Professor Yeh Chang-ching of the then Chinese Catholic University (*Fu Jen*) in Peking, had to participate in a land reform program, along with hundreds of other professors and intellectuals, as a part of their "political education." When Yeh was in Yu Kiang, a small town in south Kiangsu, he was struck with the peasants' vocabulary and noted the following words he found on the lips of every peasant in his daily conversation.[3]

1.	*ming chueh*	to understand clearly
2.	*ling tao*	to guide (verb), authorities (noun)
3.	*tou cheng*	to struggle
4.	*ya po*	oppression
5.	*mu piao*	objective
6.	*ssu hsiang*	ideology
7.	*tao lun*	discussion
8.	*jo tien*	weakness
9.	*chi chi*	aggressive
10.	*cheng tse*	policy
11.	*feng chieh shih li*	feudalistic forces
12.	*tung chih*	control
13.	*piao chun*	standard
14.	*chueh wu*	consciousness
15.	*yen chiu*	research
16.	*tsung chieh*	conclusion
17.	*che ti*	thoroughly
18.	*jen wu*	task or assignment
19.	*po hsiao chi tu*	system of exploitation
20.	*pu fa*	illegal
21.	*wen ti*	problem, issue, question
22.	*chien cha*	investigation
23.	*chiao liu*	exchange of ideas or experience
24.	*pu chung*	to supplement
25.	*kai chan*	to start or develop
26.	*tuan chieh*	unity or to unify
27.	*cheng chih wei feng*	political prestige
28.	*pao pi*	accomplice
29.	*chu yao*	most important

30. *ken chu*   according to
31. *yu tien*   advantage
32. *ho fa*   legal
33. *ho li*   logical

To one who knows Chinese, the peculiarity of such terms is remarkable. Many of them are typical Communist jargon; most of them have new connotations, unknown in pre-Communist China, although not every one of them is a Communist literary invention. Almost all of them were not expressions commonly used before by Chinese peasants.

The list was submitted to a group of twelve professors who had been born in China but who are now living in the United States. It was their opinion that only five of the expressions would conceivably have been used by peasants prior to 1949, and then only by men. They were: *ya po* (oppression), *ssu hsiang* (ideology), *wen ti* (problem, issue), *ho li* (logical) and *ho fa* (legal). None of them thought that Chinese peasants in pre-Communist days would have understood such expressions as *ling tao* (authorities), *chueh wu* (consciousness), *tsung chieh* (conclusion), *chiao liu* (exchange of ideas) or *tou cheng* (struggle).

How Chinese peasants actually feel about the connotations of these expressions is not the point here. What is important is that they had acquired a new vocabulary that symbolizes the Communist ideology. And one need not go too far in political, psychological, or sociological theories to understand why such symbolization is of extreme importance to any political or social system and why skillful manipulation of political symbols is of especial importance to Communism.

At work behind this political education of the Chinese peasants is an almost unique system of mass communication. In addition to the conventional media, which, incidentally, are utilized in an entirely different manner in China than elsewhere, the Communists depend on a variety of channels and devices that are rarely considered tools for "mass communication" as the term is understood in the United States: blackboard newspapers, *tatzepao* (handwritten posters), street-corner plays, folk dances, songs, poetry, personal communication with the "propagandists," and various means of thought reform.

Some factors in this communication system are Communist, some are traditionally Chinese, some are inventions of the Chinese Marxists. Together, they suggest something of a revolution in communication. Motivated by the general goals of Chinese Communism and guided by a new communication elite, this revolution has resulted in new images, new symbols, a new language, a new audience, new communication methods, and new communication behavior of the masses.

So mammoth is this revolution that it is difficult either to scale it down to size or explain it in simple terms. Only a few scenes of this communication revolution can be examined and only a few of the major communication media can be discussed.

Communications in a Commune

To understand some of the peculiarities of this communication system, let us take a glimpse at a small rural town in China. This is Tsao Hsien, a farming community of about 20,000 in Anhwei province. Like other rural communities in Anhwei, or, indeed, in all of China, this town in pre-Communist days probably had a large number of illiterate peasants who had little direct contact with the national government and whose activities were not always centrally or vigorously controlled. Education was no more than a matter of a few primary schools and private tutors; perhaps there were a few reading rooms and "mass education centers," but they were poorly equipped, inefficiently administered, and only occasionally utilized. There might have been a mimeographed or badly printed local paper of some kind, and a few families in the town perhaps had access to the better provincial or prestige national newspapers through the mail. There was no radio station, although a few well-to-do families perhaps owned radio sets. The moving picture was probably a strange novelty to most of the inhabitants, who depended on local talent and small traveling troupes for entertainment on special festivals or occasions. Government activity was probably rare.

But let us now turn to this town in 1959, as reported by Ho Pi, the first secretary of the Party branch in the area.[4] Tsao Hsien has now become a commune, known as the Shih Chi Commune of Tsao Hsien. It has 5,253 families (21,000 people) and a farming area of 64,000 *mu.** "Cultural work," writes Ho Pi, "has already been extended to every corner of the commune." He lists the following:

Newspaper reading groups	267
Art and Literary Teams	267
Production Research Teams	267
Cultural Association of the Communes	1
Propaganda Instrument Workshop	1
Production Agitation Board	80
Blackboard Newspapers and *Tatzepao* (posters)	390
Movie projection team	1
Libraries	17
Cultural Centers	8
Exhibition Centers	4
Recreation Centers	57
After-work Cultural Workers Corps	15
Youth Cultural Palaces	27
People's Fun Centers	4
Current Affairs and Political Propaganda Teams	35
Kiddie Dancing Teams	11
Huang Chung Dancing Teams	8
Children Dancing Teams	34
Weather Bulletins	8
Radio Station (radio diffusion exchange)	1
Local Message-relay centers	25
Primary Schools	20
After-work Middle Schools	7
"Red" and "Expert" Schools†	1
Young Farmers' Schools	1
Art Schools	4
Public Education Schools	1
Party Night Schools	7
Farmers' After-work Grade Schools	155
Youth Corps Night Schools	7
Basketball Teams	56
Volleyball Teams	2
Playgrounds	2

* *Mu* is a Chinese measurement equal to about one-sixth of an acre.

† This is a popular expression in Communist China: A person is supposed to be first of all "Red" in his ideology and also "expert" in his work.

"Most of these cultural organizations," Ho hastens to point out, "are useful for propaganda activities on a permanent basis and in a variety of ways." He goes on to explain how these "cultural organizations" have "enriched the cultural life of the masses, pushed forward production and central tasks in different periods and greatly changed the social atmosphere and cultural outwork of the people." Ho refers to this as part of a "cultural revolution" now going on in China and paints the picture in a verse:

> Poetry is all over walls and drawings are everywhere,
> Everyone goes to school, everyone has books to read;
> Like a galloping horse, we break through the cultural gate,
> And now it is on the farms where writers and poets meet.

One must not be misled into believing that the Communists are interested in this "cultural revolution" for literary or aesthetic reasons. "Poetry, songs, and wall drawings," Ho puts bluntly, "are powerful weapons to encourage production and to stimulate people to work. . . . The harder the members of the commune are working in production, the more they write poems and paint."

All this suggests that cultural work must be integrated with politics and production. This is the only way to push forward production and political struggle.

Poems and songs of the masses are the best forms of self-education. Ever since the Great Leap Forward Campaign, already 13,000 in the commune have participated in writing poetry and composing songs and more than 2,000 have done wall drawings.

According to incomplete statistics, from March, 1958, till now (less than one year), the people have produced 180,000 folk songs, 87 plays, 170 novels and short stories, 520,000 poems, 190,000 wall drawings. At the moment, members of the commune are busy writing scripts for movies and plays for stages as their way to salute the National Anniversary of 1959. Also appearing in the commune are 18 kinds of art and literature publications, including the *Shih Chi Art and Literature*, *Shih Chih Poetry and Paintings* and *Tung Feng* [*East Wind*]. Then there are also 17 other kinds of publications such as *Great Leap Forward Express* and *Tsan Tou Pao* [*Combat Paper*].

One must be cautioned about some of the terms Ho used. The word "school" may not mean any more than an organized gathering for the purpose of teaching the peasants how to read and write; a "youth culture palace" may be just a room where youth gather for propaganda and recreational activities; a "weather bulletin" may be just a blackboard with current information about the weather conditions; a "library" may be just a reading center where some propaganda literature and a few newspapers are available; a "poem" may be nothing more than a jingle or crudely composed rhymed lines.

How much truth there is in Ho's report cannot be easily ascertained. But even if only one-tenth of what he describes now exists, it is sufficiently illustrative of the Communists' attempt to utilize as many channels and forms of communication as possible to achieve their political objectives.

The System's Operation

The key link in the entire communication system is *Jen Min Jih Pao*, through which the Department of Propaganda operates and to which all papers in the nation turn for guidance and direction. In recent years, the magazine *Hung Chi* (*Red Flag*), also a mouthpiece of the Party's Central Committee, has been assigned a somewhat similar and equally important function.

What is published in *Jen Min Jih Pao* is reprinted or quoted in Party newspapers at different levels, special newspapers (such as *Worker's Daily* of the All-China Federation of Trade Unions, *Youth Daily* of the Democratic Youth Corps, etc.) and other trade, professional or special-purpose publications. Its reports are carried by the People's Broadcasting Station in Peking, which transmits them to stations in the provinces and other cities, and these stations in turn send the word further down through the radio broadcasting network which makes the message available to listeners either in collective listening meetings or in blackboard or wall newspapers. Eventually its messages are printed as booklets or pamphlets that are made available for *hsueh hsi*, or study, groups, for cultural affairs study groups, and for hundreds of other groups or occasions. (It must be noted that the *Jen Min Jih Pao* messages, unless they concern government or party directives or the like, are not always repeated verbatim. In transmitting a message from Peking, the local newspaper, magazine, or radio station normally "integrates" the message with the local situation. This is not a matter of "adding local color to the story," as an American journalist might describe it; it is done not only to relate it to the local situation but also, and mainly, to set the stage for agitation activities.)

Indeed, to read a newspaper in China today is a political obligation. Any news item that is considered important in Peking is required reading in newspaper-reading groups and "collective radio listening groups"; it is discussed at study and indoctrination meetings and may even become part of the people's "thought conclusions" or "work reports." If it is a news story about killing so many sparrows in Town A, one can be sure that the "glory" of Town A will not shine alone: Town B may be "mobilized" to kill twice as many sparrows. And, if this should be the case, there will be special meetings to discuss the methods and operation of sparrow-killing, poems composed, street-corner plays written, slogans coined, and dances planned to popularize the affair. Most certainly there will be criticism and self-criticism meetings. In no time at all, sparrow-killing will be the "central task" of Town B: school children of one class will challenge those in another to a competition; one "work brigade" tries to outdo the record of another; one member of the "propaganda network" labors to outdistance his colleagues. If the "model experience" of sparrow-killing in Town A has inspired truly remarkable activity in Town B, the successes in Town B will not go unnoticed but will be "reflected" in various communiqués to agitate other towns. The contest will continue, to stop only when another "central task" emerges. Tasks vary, but tasks there always are.

In addition to major campaigns such as Land Reform or the "Hundred Flowers," there are seasonal ones—the anniversary of the Party, of the People's Government, of the October Revolution —and campaigns inspired by special occasions for special groups. For instance, there is the Teachers' Day for Teachers and Journalists' Day for Journalists. And there are always campaigns of the sparrow-killing kind.

It may be helpful at this point to take the case of a truly major movement in order to describe how various kinds of persuasive communications are mobilized. There is no doubt that communization was the major goal of the Chinese Communist Party, even in their early days of revolution. But, remembering the cardinal principle that every campaign or movement requires class consciousness at a specific level, the Communists realized that the nation was not at first "ideologically prepared" for such a drastic move. Even when the People's Republic was proclaimed in 1949, not a whisper was heard about communization. The first years of the Republic were devoted to the Land Reform movement, then the "mutual aid groups," "collective co-ops," the campaign "to combine small co-ops into large co-ops," and the more ambitious program of "collectivization." Finally, the time was ripe for communes.

The movement for people's communes was officially inaugurated in September, 1958. Early in July, 1958, occasional stories began to appear in *Jen Min Jih Pao* suggesting the desirability of having "socialistic families." On July 6, a letter appeared from a housewife, telling the editor of the importance and joy of socialistic families and asking him to give up the idea of "selfish small families." The following day, a long piece appeared on the success of a "public mess hall" in an agricultural co-op. This was followed with another piece advocating "the development of such practices."

On August 11, the paper gave front-page coverage to Mao Tsetung's inspection tour in Honan, where he had lavishly praised the performance of a "commune" there. "As long as we have a commune like this, there will be more communes," Mao was quoted. (The commune at Hsing-yang in Honan was one of the Communists' major experiments. What was done there was reported and popularized extensively, not only to inspire the nation but also to demonstrate it as a "model" to be followed.) Two days later, Mao was in Shantung and the paper headlined Mao's statement: "We should do well with communes. The advantage: to unite workers, peasants, merchants, intellectuals, and soldiers. Such a system will facilitate political guidance." By the middle of August, when the Politburo was reportedly meeting at Pai Tai Ho, stories suddenly mushroomed in *Jen Min Jih Pao*. There was a long article about a commune in Hsing-yang, Honan (August 18), another about one in Sinkiang (August 16), Chekiang (August 18), and Tientsin (August 19).

Then, on September 1, a front-page story appeared that the Enlarged Conference of the Party's Political Bureau had decided to announce the "great objective of producing 170.7 million tons of steel and of making the people's commune the best form to accelerate the transitional period from socialism to communism." But, the story insisted, "The establishment of people's communes must be made on the basis of the initial consciousness of the masses. It must be done through discussions and indoctrination of the masses as done in the Hundred Flowers movement."

Then came the final official notice, which *Jen Min Jih Pao* front-paged on September 10–"Decisions of the Central Committee of the Chinese Communist Party on the Problem of Establishing People's Communes." (It is significant that the Central Committee's decision was made on August 29, but the official announcement of it not until September 10.)

Weeks before the publication of the official announcement, however, the movement was already being carried out in the nation "with fanfare." One needs only the opening paragraph of an editorial in *Jen Min Jih Pao* of September 3 to see how vigorously persuasive communications were already at work:

> People's communes which symbolize a new period of our socialist movement in the rural area, are now established very swiftly in various areas. . . . The movement was started as a result of the high level of socialistic consciousness of the masses. After a few early communes obtained their success, many agricultural co-ops began to study such models and thus started the movement. . . . Peasants in many areas have written huge volumes of *Tatzepao* (posters), petitions and letters to express their determination; they requested to establish people's communes.

To be sure that all the propaganda authorities in the nation would carry out their task efficiently, *Jen Min Jih Pao* released on September 11 "Propaganda and Education Directive of the Central Committee of the Chinese Communist Party." The five-point Directive spelled out the meaning of the movement, the propaganda content, the methods to be used, the arguments to be advanced, and the steps to be followed. It emphasized: "From the beginning to the end, this movement must follow the principles of settling contradictions among People*; it should make use of confessions, accusations, debates, discussions, *tatzepao*, demonstration meetings, exhibits and all kinds of forms to achieve genuine ideological liberation and to make the movement a REAL, BROAD MOVEMENT OF SELF-EDUCATION."

By this time, the movement had reached its zenith. Before the end of the year, *Jen Min Jih Pao* reported (on December 31), "Agricultural co-ops are already a thing of the past in the rural areas of our country. According to our statistics for November, 99.1 per cent of our peasants have already 26,500 big and fair people's communes which include 126.9 million families. In average, every commune has about 4,756 families."

While it should be fairly easy to imagine the role of the conventional mass media in the propaganda campaign of the Communization movement, it is perhaps necessary to add a word here regarding some of the informal ones. "Discussion meetings," for instance, is one such medium. The following story, which appeared in the November 18, 1959, issue of *Jen Min Jih Pao,* illustrates its dramatic use:

> Rural areas in Hupeh are now engaged in a broad and penetrating Communist educational movement. During this movement, people in different areas make use of big discussion meetings to criticize the existing capitalistic ideologies of the minority cadres and middle peasants.
>
> When the Satellite Team of the Welfare Commune of Hung-an Country was engaging in its discussion in the field, a new middle peasant Hsiang Chien-kwei said: "People's communes are good. There is one thing wrong: you don't have enough to eat." Poor peasant Cheng Kwei-ying began to argue with him: "You forget your pain after you've lost your scar; you forget about the well-digger after you've got your water. You used to have foodless days or days without three square meals. You've forgotten about all that. I'll say: People's communes are wonderful. There is more rice than you can finish."

---

* This is a reference to the Communist experience of ideological rectification following the "Hundred Flowers" movement of 1957, and especially to the important article written by Mao on this subject.

Hsiang would not accept the argument. Moreover, he began to ridicule Cheng. Cheng then asked Hsiang to recall all the changes that have happened to him since Land Reform and made Hsiang finally confess his mistakes. Hsiang was so moved that he wrote several copies of *tatzepao* which he left on Cheng's door.

What Hsiang wrote on the *tatzepao* was a poem, in which he slapped his face for being "so ungrateful to the Communist Party," expressed his gratitude to Cheng for "educating" him, confessed his stupidity for still harboring capitalistic ideology, and pledged to became a "new Communist man."

6. MASS COMMUNICATION: THE PRESS

When George Stafford Gale, correspondent for *The Guardian* (Manchester), accompanied the British Labour delegation on a trip to Red China in 1954, he reported that he had met "at least a hundred Chinese journalists." About them, Gale wrote, "I remember that not one of them ever asked any question, that not one of them ever started a conversation, and that not one of them was capable of discussing the matter of free speech."[1] He tried more than once in various cities to discuss with the journalists the problem of freedom of the press, but the conversation always went like this:

"Can you criticize the Government?" I would ask.

"Of course we can. The Press in China is quite free," the Chinese journalist would reply.

"Do you?"

"Oh, we frequently draw attention to some inefficiency of a bureaucrat, or make some recommendation that might be carried out."

"Criticizing a bureaucrat is not criticizing the Government."

"He is part of the Government, and if he does not do his job properly then it is our duty to criticize him."

"Your duty?"

"Yes, in the same way as it is our duty to tell the truth."

"But are you able to criticize the Government's policy? The major items that it lays down, I mean? Not an individual bureaucrat?"

"I have said, we are free to do so."

"Do you?"

"You do not understand. The programme has been laid down, the Common Programme. It is the people's choice. They want that programme. Our Government is carrying out that programme. What is there for us to criticize?"

"But suppose the Government wants to make a change in the programme. Would you support the change?"

"I suppose so. You see, our Government is the Government of the people, and if it wanted to change some particular part of the programme then it must be for the good of the people."

The British journalist could have spared himself such agonizing frustration if he had only equipped himself with some knowledge of the role of the press in a Communist society. Lenin made that role clear when he said that the press should be "a collective propagandist, a collective agitator, and a collective organizer."[2] His definition is quoted constantly in almost all Communist discussions of the press.

Apparently inspired by this Leninist doctrine and possibly trying even to elaborate it, Mao assigned, in a letter to two of his journalistic comrades, five major functions to the provincial press. They are: "to organize, to stimulate, to agitate, to criticize, and to propel"[3]:

1. To organize is accurately to propagate the objectives, policies and directives of the Party; it is to mobilize and organize all people into a powerful force to realize and to struggle for the various great tasks prescribed by the Party at different stages in history.

2. To develop fully the function of agitation and stimulation, editors must wholeheartedly integrate the creativeness of the masses with their emotions and energy to reflect accurately and timely the accomplishments of the various fronts; they should further learn to make use of the experience of the people's success to suggest new demands, to agitate the masses to compete with or challenge those who have gained early successes.

3. The most important function of criticism of the press is to be able to select issues and to present convincing arguments to attack the various shades of opportunism, conservation and destructive capitalism, to assure the establishment of socialism, to conquer pessimism and to mobilize aggressivism.

Another definition of the role of the press was offered by Lu Ting-i, director of the Department of Propaganda. "The press," he stated, "is an instrument of class struggle," as is the Party, the government, the army, the court or the school, "all weapons used by the proletarian class to overthrow capitalism and to build up socialism."[4] Teng Kuo, Editor of *Jen Min Jih Pao*, considers the press "the most powerful and effective weapon to mobilize and organize the broad masses for the building of socialism, particularly the fight for agricultural production and struggle against nature."[5] To him, a journalist is above all a fighter or warrior: "The journalistic battle front is the front where the sharpest and fiercest political ideological battles are fought."[6]

The responsibilities of a journalist in Communist China, therefore, bear little resemblance to those of his counterparts in a democracy. His main job, to be blunt, is propaganda. Journalism majors in Shanghai's Futan University are taught that journalistic work is the "heavy industry in the realm of ideological indoctrination."[7]

Only a few months after the Communists took over the Chinese mainland, a National Press Meeting was called in March, 1950, and a four-point directive was issued to newspapers, news agencies, broadcasting stations, and other news media:

1. Newspapers should devote more space and give prominence to reports on the progress of the people's labor and production, publicizing the experiences of success as well as the lessons of error derived from the work of production and financial and economic tasks, and discussing methods of overcoming difficulties in such tasks.

2. Newspapers should reorganize their functional structure in such a way that direction and management would be centralized in the hands of the editors.

3. Newspapers should consider the establishment and direction of "correspondent networks and newspaper-reading" groups as their major political tasks.

4. Newspapers should assume responsibility for criticism of the weaknesses or mistakes of the governmental agencies, economic organization, and government personnel; but such criticisms should be truthful and constructive. They should pay the greatest attention to the handling of letters to the editor.[8]

The first point of the directive, dealing with the content of the press, with propaganda for socialism and Communism, and with agitation for production, is definitely a point derived from the Soviet experience:

In the earliest days of the Soviet regime, Lenin declared that it was a fundamental necessity "to transform the press from an organ which primarily reports the political news of the day into a serious organ for economic education of the mass of the population." . . . Lenin offered the Soviet newspapers the slogan of "less politics and more economics," and he made it clear that when he spoke of economics he did not mean theoretical arguments, learned reviews, and highbrow plans, which he labeled "twaddle." Instead he demanded that more attention be paid to the workaday aspects of factory, village and military life. The principal task of the press in the period of transition from capitalism to communism, Lenin asserted, was to train the masses for the tasks of building the new society, and this meant that the newspapers must give first place to labor problems and to their immediate practical resolution.[9]

Even a quick glance at the newspapers in Communist China reveals that news stories and feature articles about the production activities and economic life of the peasants and workers flood the columns. This is especially true in provincial and local newspapers where news, as it is understood in the Western world, is kept to a minimum. This is not to say that the Chinese Communists are not interested in news. It is only to suggest that to them, news can be about only one thing: the process of developing socialism and eventually Communism. This is their concept of "news." It is in this context that "news" is presented. And this is how news media are utilized to aid the political development of the country.

While it is only natural for the Communist Party, motivated by an entirely new ideology, to introduce totally new editorial content, it was probably not to be expected that methods of writing, printing, circulating, and reading newspapers were to be revolutionized also.

Chinese Communist newspapers are so different from the traditional ones that even a well-educated Chinese scholar, unless he has been following the Communist press for the past few years, is likely not to understand everything that is printed in them. To begin with, he will be surprised or even irritated to discover that they are now printed in horizontal lines, as in English, instead of in the traditionally vertical arrangement. But he will be appalled by what was traditionally considered an unforgivably illiterate use of ideograms. Ideas that are, in traditional written Chinese, expressed by different characters but pronounced in the same way, are now represented by one character which is the easiest to write —as if the word "site" in English, for instance, were used whenever "cite," "sight," or "site" was meant. If this "misspelling" appalls our traditional Chinese reader, his agony will increase when he encounters some of the old Chinese characters that are now so simplified in their written form as to defy recognition. He will have even more excruciating moments with some of the new Communist expressions. He may not be able to make out some of them, such as the currently popular *hsia fang kan pu*, which means dispatching cadres to the countryside or factories "in order to study the wisdom of the masses." He may not be able to bear the new use of such expressions as *ai jen*, or "lover," which husbands and wives now use to refer to each other in public.

But these are only changes in the Chinese language, and this is not where the revolution in Chinese newspapers ends.

In Communist China, where "correctness in thinking" is now believed to be far more important in any task than technical competence, writing is no longer the monopoly of the intellectuals. It is thus not at all unusual to find newspaper stories written by "correspondents" who can barely read or write, poems composed by those who hardly know the fundamentals of the language, and plays produced by those who are almost illiterate.

The establishment of "correspondence networks" is similar to the Soviet *Rabssel'kor*, the Worker and Peasant Correspondent Movement. A "correspondent" is any man or woman, in factory or field, who writes to newspapers about his work, his economic life, his experience in political study, and the accomplishments or failures of those around him. Writing ability is a matter of secondary importance. In a book entitled "How to Write Newspaper Correspondence," the following is stressed:

> Many comrades believe that to write for newspapers is the task of intellectuals and not related to themselves. This is a wrong attitude. If you are a Communist Party member and revolutionary cadre, then you have the responsibility of writing stories for Party newspapers or papers of the masses. If you are at a very low level of il-

literacy and do not know how to write, you can learn slowly. But you must never pass on the responsibility which is yours to somebody else.[10]

Less than a year after the Communist victory on the Chinese mainland, most newspapers already claimed to have a huge army of correspondents. In 1950, *Ho Pei Jih Pao* (*Hopei Daily*) claimed to have 1,600 correspondents; *Fu Kien Jih Pao* (*Fukien Daily*) 5,000; and *Lao Tun Pao* (*Labor Daily*) as many as 7,000.[11]

How the "correspondents" help the propaganda function of the Party is explicitly revealed in an official report in which the following statement from *Nung Ming Pao* (*Farmer's Daily*) in Shensi is quoted:

> It has been verified by our experience that only by depending upon correct propaganda policies can our task of uniting closely with the masses be lively, and that only by tying together the actual life and work of the masses with propaganda can our policies be convincing and effective. We have come to understand that peasants have the following habit in comprehension and understanding: they will not accept a theory or principle if it is not coupled with "facts"; but they cannot see through the "facts" if no "reason" or "theory" is given and therefore cannot raise their level of consciousness. To make newspaper articles appealing and convincing and to strengthen the effect of newspaper propaganda, there must be actual examples together with convincing arguments. Therefore, we will not merely deal with vague facts that are not well organized.[12]

The "correspondence network" movement is also regarded as a method of training journalists for the Communist press. But above all, it is supposed to serve as the eyes and ears of the press and Party in every area of the nation's life. It is this latter aspect of their work that integrates the correspondents with the institution of self-criticism.

Perhaps even more important than the "correspondence network" are the "newspaper-reading groups," where the news is read aloud and discussed. Newspaper reading is an important political obligation for practically everyone in China today; it is the "major cultural and educational activity" in factories and villages. Even fifth-graders in a Peking elementary school are "organized to read newspapers." "In this particular school," reports a Peking evening paper, "the leadership and the Youth Volunteers are extremely interested in utilizing youth newspapers to engage in political and ideological education among students."[13] The usefulness of these groups is not difficult to understand: First, it forces the illiterate to "read" the newspapers; second, it forces the educated man not only to read the papers, but to explain the news to others who cannot; third, it enables oral agitators to do their work while discussion of the news takes place.

Another major responsibility of the press is the intensive practice of criticism and self-criticism. Since the practice of criticism is supposed to work from top to bottom and from bottom to top, it is natural that the press is used as a transmission belt between the Party and the government on the one hand and the masses of the people on the other.

Natural or not, however, the assignment of responsibility for self-criticism to the press is significant. As early as 1950, the Central Committee of the Party issued a special directive on the subject. Government officials charged with press affairs were supposed "to help newspapers and publications to distinguish constructive from malicious or destructive criticisms."[14] These officials usually belong to the Party and to provincial and local government agencies, but they are also under the supervision and guidance of central Party and government authorities. The control of newspapers by the Party and government is therefore complete, from the central agencies in Peking to the lowest levels.

It is difficult to determine how many newspapers and magazines are actually published in Communist China or how large the circulation. Only scanty information on the matter has been released by the Communists. According to figures released by the Minister of Culture Shen Yen-ping, at the first session of the Second National People's Congress in 1959, Communist China published "1,884 newspapers, with a [total] circulation of 4,899,-990,000 copies; 818 magazines, with a circulation of 537,050,000 copies; as well as 46,018 books totaling 2,393,090,000 copies."[15] But according to information gathered by the American Consulate General in Hong Kong, there were in 1955 only "88 newspapers that had been identified as being published regularly on the mainland." This number "increased to 142 in 1956 and as of

October 1, 1957, it stands at 822 papers known to be published on the Chinese mainland." On the other hand, the Consulate General reported that 62 papers had ceased publication or changed names when the above information was compiled.[16]

There is little doubt that the number of newspapers in Communist China has increased and that the total circulation is probably larger than before. But the official figures released by Communist China in 1959 seem unbelievably high. One research source, for instance, presented in 1961 the following picture:

> At present, the average newspaper on the country level has a reported circulation of several hundred copies per issue, although newspapers with wider geographical bases generally have a larger circulation. In fact, some of the nation's leading newspapers print more than 100,000 copies daily. As of June, 1958, the total circulation of all newspapers printed in the country was 15 copies per issue, almost a five-fold increase over the 3 million copies per issue in 1951. There is now one newspaper for every 40 persons, whereas the ratio in 1951 was one to every 274 persons.[17]

Understandably, the most important newspapers are those published by the Party, which are under the control of the Commission on Party Press of the Central Committee. There are mouthpieces for special organizations—the labor unions, New Democratic Youth Corps, and other so-called mass organizations. There are also "non-Communist" newspapers such as the *Kuang Ming Jih Pao*, which claims to speak for "democratic parties," even "private" newspapers such as the once-famous *Ta Kung Pao* and *Hsin Min Pao*, both in Shanghai. But all these strictly follow the "Party line," just as all the Party newspapers do.

The Party newspapers deserve special attention here because they form the major channels through which the Party transmits its daily messages to the people. These papers, to borrow a Communist expression, "contribute to widening the ideological, political, cultural and educational horizon of the masses." They not only provide the masses with the "correct" interpretations of Marxism-Leninism and Maoism but also "facilitate their study of current affairs, politics and economics, their problems of today and their hopes of tomorrow."

No Chinese newspaper is, of course, more powerful than *Jen Min Jih Pao*. Whenever the Party or government initiates a movement or campaign, *Jen Min Jih Pao* is normally the first paper to elucidate the significance of the issue from the Marxist-Leninist viewpoint and to map out plans to push forward the movement. It is also *Jen Min Jih Pao* that will keep posted on the development of the movement and point out its accomplishments and weaknesses. Its editorials and special articles are constantly reprinted by newspapers all over the country, particularly the papers put out by the regional bureaus and sub-bureaus of the Central Committee. Such papers include: *Chieh Fang Jih Pao* (*Liberation Daily*, Shanghai); *Ch'ang Chiang Jih Pao* (*Yangtze Daily*, Hankow); *Nan Fang Jih Pao* (*Southern Daily*, Canton); *Tung Pei Jih Pao* (*Northeast Daily*, Mukden); *Ch'ün Chung Jih Pao* (*Daily of the Masses*, Sian); *Lu Ta Jen Min Jih Pao* (*People's Daily*, Port Arthur and Dairen); *Fukien Jih Pao* (*Fukien Daily*, Foochow) and; *Tientsin Jih Pao* (*Tientsin Daily*).

But what does *Jen Min Jih Pao* look like? What kind of news does it print? Is it like *Pravda* or the *Daily Worker*? How does it differ from American or Soviet newspapers?

Jen Min Jih Pao is often described as the Chinese *Pravda*, and while this description is not inaccurate, the paper means more to Peking than *Pravda* does to Moscow. Moscow has *Pravda* as the Party newspaper and *Izvestia* as the government mouthpiece; in Peking, *Jen Min Jih Pao* speaks in theory for the Chinese Communist Party, but in reality for the People's Government of China.*

Though powerful as a political instrument, *Jen Min Jih Pao* is puny in volume and drab in appearance. During its early years, it was only four pages long, occasionally eight pages. On July 1, 1956, the paper announced its plan to "expand" to eight pages, with the following general make-up:

Page 1	Current News
Pages 2 and 3	National Economic News
Page 4	National Political News
Pages 5 and 6	International News

* For a description of the function and role of *Jen Min Jih Pao*, as they are actually described in China, see the Appendix, which gives the text of an article published in *People's China* concerning *Jen Min Jih Pao*.

Page 7	Educational and Cultural News
Page 8, upper half	A literary supplement
Page 8, lower half	Advertising

Until 1962, this eight-page plan was followed fairly consistently. In 1963, however, the paper became a six-page affair, occasionally reduced to four or expanded to eight. Whether this was in line with the Communist austerity policy or the result of a shortage of newsprint has not been officially explained. In any case, *Jen Min Jih Pao*, though smaller than most weekly papers in the United States, is much larger than other newspapers in the Chinese mainland. For a four-page daily is the standard one in Communist China today; even the once-famous *Ta Kung Pao* rarely prints a larger issue.

But the size of Chinese Communist newspapers is a relatively minor matter. Obviously, what a newspaper prints is far more important than how many pages it prints. Limitations of space do not permit an extended discussion here of the distinctive features of *Jen Min Jih Pao*. But it may suffice to present here the contents of a single issue—the one for March 18, 1963, selected more or less at random. What follows are the headlines of all the news stories, features, and graphic material appearing in that issue. They are faithful line-by-line translations of the original Chinese, preserving as much as possible of the tone, expression, and flavor of Peking journalism. The issue is a typical one in its handling of news and headline style. (Chinese Communist editors have their own unique style for writing headlines, which has little in common with that used either in traditional Chinese newspapers or in present-day Chinese publications in Taiwan. Many of the headlines are notoriously long—so long that they were even attacked by Communist editors themselves, and rather severely, during the "Hundred Flowers" campaign of 1957.) It is not at all uncommon for special slogans to appear as headlines in bold-face or large types, around and under which special stories will be grouped. Sometimes the same slogans are used for several days. And, not infrequently, there will be no news stories, as the genre is understood in the United States, on the front page. When Peking and Moscow decided to hold a conference to discuss what are commonly described as their ideological differences, the entire front page of the March 14, 1963, issue was devoted to the texts of the letters written by the two Communist parties; no news dispatch or story appeared. Nor is it unusual for *Jen Min Jih Pao* to fill its entire front page with a long speech by Mao Tse-tung delivered as early as 1925 or 1931. Such reprints, in fact, take up several pages and leave only the back pages for news items and editorial columns.

Jen Min Jih Pao, March 18, 1963

Page 1.

Comrades Mao, Liu, Chou, Teng
Yesterday Received Delegates to Five Conferences

[Not a long story, but accompanied by a large picture showing Mao, Liu, Chou, and Teng Hsiao-ping (Vice-Premier and Secretary General of the Party) receiving unidentified delegates.]

With Relatively Sufficient Preparation for Plowing; With Timely Shipment of Equipment for Springtime Plowing
Szechuan Basin Area Blessed by Rain and Busy With Springtime Plowing

[One of the major campaigns in Communist China is the seeding and plowing during the spring. Stories like this one are run in almost all major newspapers.]

Cadres in the Rural Areas in Kirin Learn from Liu Hsi-ting
Be A Good Leader; Have A Good Production Team
Liu Hsi-ting is a Member of the Production Team in Tung-Hua County (in Kirin). Selfless, Capable of Following the Mass Line and Paying Attention to Cut Expenses, He is Able to Lead All Members of his Commune to Change the Whole Picture of Production in One Year.

Marshal Lin Piao Sends Greetings on the Anniversary of Armed Forces of the Mongolian People

Proved by the Ten-Year Experience of the Shansi Branch of the Academy of the Chinese Agricultural Science:
There are Many Advantages for Institutions of Agricultural Science to Establish Research Posts in Villages

Many Research Organizations of Agricultural Science
and Institutions of Higher Education in Peking
Have Established Research Stations in Rural
Areas to Strengthen the Ties in Production

[That research stations must be established in rural areas for the study of agricultural science is perhaps obvious to Americans. But in China, scholars and professors who spend more time on the university campus than in rural areas, are accused of being unfamiliar with conditions on the farms. The purpose of such stories is to make intellectuals "learn from peasants." It is part of Peking's long-range plan to elevate the status of the peasants and to mobilize intellectuals "to enrich their experience in production and revolution" by "going to the midst of the toiling masses."]

U.S. Gunboats Trespass Coastal Area of Fukien
We Issue the 235th Serious Warning

[This is only a two-inch story printed at the bottom of the page. That the 235th "Serious Warning" is issued suggests that all previous warnings were reported dutifully and frequently. While it is easy to understand Peking's intention in printing stories such as this one, it is hard to know how they are interpreted by the readers. Do they brand the United States as aggressors, as such stories are intended to suggest? Or do they believe that their rulers were actually intimidated by the "paper tiger," since the government took no stronger action than issuing "serious warnings"?]

Page 2.

Lei Feng's Fighting Comrades Remember Lei Feng
Exhibition of Comrade Lei Feng's Heroic Deeds Scheduled to Open in Peking

[One major campaign in early 1963 was the "Movement to Study from Lei Feng." Eulogized as the "glorious Communist Warrior," Lei Feng was suddenly discovered to be a model soldier. His diary, widely publicized, is full of praises for the Chinese Communist Party and other passages that suggest his dedication to the Party.]

The Art of Lecturing in a Class
On Wang Chi-Hsien, a Language Teacher in a Primary School

Hsu Kai-Tsai of the People's Liberation Army
Sets Two New Records in Archery

Inner Mongolia is Busy With Seeding and Spring Plowing
Southern Tibet Starts its Spring Plowing Program
Acreage of Sesame Planting Enlarged in Hupeh

Spring in the Countryside

[Five pictures about a place in the province of Chekiang, with these captions: "Chien Mei People's Commune Makes Preparation for Spring Plowing"; "To Send Fertilizer to the Country"; "To Select Carefully Quality Seeds"; "To Plant Trees in the Mountain"; "To Repair Agricultural Instruments." All the pictures are reprinted from the *Chekiang Jih Pao* (*Chekiang Daily News*). The photographs obviously suggest the types of chores which are urged by the government.]

Page 3.

Diem's Biggest "Annihilation" Campaign this Year Again a Failure
South Vietnamese People Counterattack Heroically,
Win Victory

[This story is accompanied by two photographs, one showing the "strategic outposts" and another showing U.S. rifles captured by Communists.]

South Rhodesian People are Determined to Fight for Their Independence

Ruling Classes Depend upon Violence to Suppress People and to Resist the High Tide of Revolution
Military Uprising is the Only Road that Leads to a Thorough Socialistic Reconstruction
Ecuador's Revolutionary Youth Daily *Comments on the Future of Ecuador*

Indian Newspapers Urge Break-up of Talks with China
India Calls for Speedy Expansion of Armed Forces and Preparation for War
U.S. Military Weapons Still Arrive in Indian Ports

Different Circles in Pakistan Issue Statements
The Sino-Pakistani Agreement Warmly Received
Pointing out that the Signing of the Agreement Between China and Afghanistan is Another Step Forward in Establishing Long-term Friendly Neighborly Relationships

King of Laos Arrives in Burma on State Visit
De Gaulle Visits The Netherlands Hastily
Peking's Vaudeville Group in Tokyo
[A long feature article giving a glowing report of the "enthusiastic" reception given the Communist Vaudeville Group in Japan.]

Brief International News Items:
27,000 Greek Handicraft Workers on Strike
Pedicab Drivers on Strike in New Delhi
Armed Peru Group Attacks Police Station
U.S. Army Commander of Armed Forces in the Pacific Area is Active in Thailand
Another Wave of U.S. "Peace Corps" Arrives in Bolivia
More than One Million Traffic Accidents Reported in West Germany Last Year

Page 4.
[Five literary pieces.]
Spring in Tsou-Chow and Swatow, by Ho Lung
The Most Beautiful Verses, by Huang Shih-heng
[Another piece about Lei Feng, the much publicized "Glorious Communist Warrior." Apparently, Lei wrote some poems which were included in his widely circulated diary. In this piece, Lei's "devotion" to the Party is once again cited as the quality all people in China are urged to acquire.]

In Memory of Comrade Cheng Nien-Chiu Who Fought Long and Hard
[Cheng was a famous Peking opera singer, who was best known for his singing and playing of female roles. This piece was written to commemorate the fifth anniversary of his death.]

Springtime in the Mountain
[The caption for a line drawing done by a member of the Chinghai Quick Sketch Group.]

The Glory of Morning Sun
[*Five short poems.*]

> [The bottom one-third of this page is devoted to so-called advertisements. One large advertisement is for new books published by different branches of the New China Bookstore; one is a small public announcement of the exhibition of the "Model and Glorious Deeds of Lei Feng"; another small advertisement is for an important Communist economics magazine; the last two short advertisements are both for government publishing companies. As one can readily see, there is no commercial advertising.]

Generally speaking, most of the dailies in Communist China today are not very different from *Jen Min Jih Pao* in appearance or content. Compare, for instance, the April 18, 1963, issues of three dailies in Peking: *Kuang Ming Jih Pao*, the official organ of the Democratic League; *Ta Kung Pao*, once the most respected and feared liberal newspaper in pre-Communist days; and *Kung Jen Jih Pao* (*Workers' Daily*), mouthpiece of the All-China Federation of Trade Unions. The most important event of April 18 happened to be a rally to welcome an important Cuban visitor. In typical Communist style, "The Meeting of All Circles of People in Peking to Assist the Cuban and all Latin American People" was organized, speeches were made by the visitor and by relevant high-ranking Chinese officials, a demonstration was staged, resolutions to support Cuba were passed, and cables were sent to Castro to assure him of the support of all China. All three newspapers devoted more than a page to coverage of this meeting. There were the predictable items: a long speech by the visiting Cuban; an equally long speech by Deputy Premier Kuo Mo-jo; the telegram sent under the name of the special rally to Fidel Castro and the Latin American people; pictures; and, in the case of *Kuang Ming Jih Pao*, an editorial.

The three papers had another full page of identical material on a "Diagram of Calisthenics." Apparently a special radio program on calisthenics was staged by the Central People's Broadcasting Station in Peking, and listeners were mobilized to improve their physical fitness. The Peking dailies had to devote a full page of their already limited space to this government-inspired campaign. *Kung Jen Jih Pao* (*Workers' Daily*) went one step further and carried an editorial on the subject.

To be sure, all three newspapers also carried special news stories designed to satisfy their own readers. But on days like April 18, 1963, such stories do not receive much attention.

A casual glance at the Communist newspapers in the early months of 1963 reveals a high degree of similarity. They all carry the news dispatches supplied by the *Hsin Hua She,* or the New China News Agency, and they normally ran all the same stories that were apparently considered important by the Party. But this similarity seems to be a fairly recent phenomenon. It became noticeable after the "Hundred Flowers" campaign, when a large number of "rightist journalists" (both Communist and non-Communist) had been severely reprimanded and much criticism of the Party press loudly voiced.

Soon after the Communist takeover in 1949, quite a few non-Communist newspapers continued their traditional operations, although they were understandably and overwhelmingly enthusiastic about the new regime. *Ta Kung Pao* did not change its makeup or writing style, and *Kuang Ming Jih Pao* continued to cater to the taste of Chinese intellectuals. A few evening newspapers, such as *Hsin Min Pao* in Nanking, continued to have a large number of human-interest stories and to specialize in its particular brand of "soft news." All these papers carried quite a bit of advertising.

Gradually, the Communist Party extended its influence over the press. By 1951 or 1952, it was quite apparent that many non-Communist newspapers had already lost their identity of pre-Communist days and that *Jen Min Jih Pao* would set the pace for all journalists in the country. That many Chinese journalists, particularly non-Communists, were unhappy with *Jen Min Jih Pao* as overlord, became dramatically clear in 1957 when a fierce battle to "oust the rightist elements on the journalistic front" was waged by the Communists in the "Hundred Flowers" movement. For several months, hardly a day passed without some journalists or newspapers being singled out for their "anti-party," "rightist," "reactionary," "anti-people," or "bourgeois" attitudes or practices. What happened to *Kuang Ming Jih Pao* and its top editorial staff members was typical.

Started in 1949 as the official mouthpiece of the Democratic League, *Kuang Ming Jih Pao* had actually served the Chinese Communist Party more efficiently than might have been expected. In 1952, a sweeping reorganization of the paper, apparently initiated or at least inspired by the Communists, resulted in a new Communist editor and "administrative committee" that were both ready and willing to carry out the wishes of the Party. All other important persons on the paper, though non-Communists, were high-ranking officials in the government: Chang Po-chun, Vice-Chairman of the China Democratic League and Minister of Communication; Lo Lung-chi, a founder of the Democratic League and later Minister of the Timber Industry; Chu An-ping, a long-time journalist in Shanghai and for several years a leading and trusted editor of several Communist publications including *Hsin Chien She* (*New Construction*). But to the surprise and disappointment of the Party, Chu An-ping evidently took too seriously Mao's call for more liberal policies and believed that he actually had some special "flowers" to grow.

In April, 1957, the paper took a leading part in a conference that demanded "complete independence and self-determination" from the control of the Party. The Party faction on the staff suffered considerable setbacks, and Chu An-ping emerged as a winner in the early stage of the game: He became the new editor. A few months later, he made a public statement entitled "Let Me Offer Some Opinions to Chairman Mao and Premier Chou," and attacked the arrogance of the Communist Party and even questioned: "Isn't it too much that within the scope of the nation there must be a Party man as leader in every unit, big or small, section or sub-section; or that nothing, big or small, can be done without a nod from the Party man?"

The Party did not act immediately. But soon enough, Chu An-ping was relieved of several of his important posts. He was even condemned by his own son, who wrote to another newspaper to accuse him. The whole editorial department of *Kuang Ming Jih Pao* had special meetings to "investigate" the mistakes of Chu,

Chang Po-chun and others.[18] The whole affair ended in a way that surprised no one: Chu confessed and apologized to the Party and to the people.[19] So did Lo Lung-chi.[20] And so did Chang Po-chun.[21] In 1958, *Kuang Ming Jih Pao* was taken over completely and became a "nation-wide government newspaper."

But Chu's story is only one of many casualties in the "rectification" that followed the "Hundred Flowers" campaign. Even in the Party's Department of Propaganda, as many as seven "rightists," including Party members, were exposed at one time.[22]

By 1958, the Party's control over all newspapers in China was complete. When Wang Mo, Deputy Director of the Section of Journalism and Publications of the Department of Propaganda, preached formally in January, 1958, that the "Party's leadership in the press is the only correct leadership" and that "the leadership of the Party is the soul of journalism in a socialistic country," no voice of challenge was raised.[23] He made it abundantly clear that no newspaper in the country could or should be free from the control of the Party:

> There are those rightists who want only limited Party leadership in journalism. They accept the leadership in terms of policies, but resist the leadership in terms of organization. They want the Party to give the orders or to specify the policies; but they do not want the Party to control the newspaper personnel. It must be understood that all policies of the Party can be carried out only through the organization of the Party and only through trustworthy and capable personnel.[24]

There is every reason to believe that the Party is now confident of its control of journalism. But whether the press continues to be an efficient instrument of persuasion in its hands can be something else entirely. If the Party has succeeded in silencing almost all voices of opposition, it has also so intimidated its journalists that their main concern is no longer the thought of being useful to the government in any original or imaginative way, but rather the desire to do only the correct things in the proper approved manner.

Hsin Hua She (New China News Agency)

Anyone who follows news from or about Communist China has noted that almost all news stories are the work of one news agency, the New China News Agency, aptly described as "the Party's eyes and tongue" by Lu Ting-i, Director of the Department of Propaganda. The NCNA is a state-owned news agency, operating as a unit of the government. Understandably, however, control of editorial policy and personnel is in the hands of the Party's Department of Propaganda. The NCNA has a virtual monopoly over news: With the possible exception of a few items of local interest gathered by reporters on individual papers, almost all news stories and articles appearing in the Chinese Communist press today come from its offices.

The NCNA began its existence under its present name in 1937, but its history goes back to 1929, when it operated as the Red China Agency first in Juichin, Kiangsi, and later in Yenan, Shensi. In 1949, the NCNA was already a rather large organization, with twelve branches and fifty-seven sub-branches in China as well as eight branches abroad. Each branch or sub-branch office had a good deal of autonomy in editorial policy, but the determination of general policy was in the hands of the head office. This division of power was, of course, understandable in a situation marked by the confusions of war and other difficulties.[25]

In 1950, however, the Party acted swiftly to streamline the NCNA operation and to centralize the control of all branch and sub-branch offices. Henceforth, branches and sub-branches only gathered information to report it to the Peking office, which screened and edited all stories before sending them back to the branches and sub-branches for publication. The central office is therefore assured of control over the information that will appear in all Chinese newspapers.

To be sure, this is a cumbersome way of gathering and distributing news, and it necessarily involves delay, making it difficult for newspapers to exploit news stories with a limited time value. But timeliness is hardly a matter of concern to the Chinese Marxists, who are interested only in getting the "correct" information into the press.

Apparently, the operation was not all smooth and efficient during the first few years after the reorganization. In a letter to all branches and sub-branches,[26] the head office at Peking had to admit that the news stories and articles it received were not all useful for nationwide publication. Only one-third of the material could be used for national release and the rest was useful only for reference. The letter charged that journalists and editors in the branches and sub-branches did not understand that "the main function and duty of the New China News Agency is to engage in propaganda to the whole nation," and that they consequently failed to write their stories in such a way that they could be effectively used by all newspapers in the country.[27]

Similar criticisms were frequently voiced during 1957, when the "Hundred Flowers" campaign was in full blossom. Though commonly brushed aside as "unjustified attacks" by "bourgeois elements" or "rightists," such criticisms suggest that the Communists had yet to overcome some of these difficulties. For instance, the fact that only "correct" information was to be disseminated led Chou Cheng, one of NCNA's staff members, to observe that three kinds of news bothered journalists most: "Things that the Party is not willing to discuss, things that the Party finds awkward to discuss, and things that the Party will not permit to be discussed."[28] Chou's criticism was described as not only outrageous but dangerous, and the explanation for it was that Chou was educated in America.

Little information is available on the actual operation of the NCNA, except that it maintains bureaus or sub-bureaus in various provinces, capitals of autonomous regions, and army units, as well as 20 or 30 foreign bureaus.

One student of Communist propaganda reports that the output of the NCNA in 1957 can be divided into five categories[29]:

1. To domestic papers on the national level and broadcasting stations all over the country, 62,000 words per day (18,000 words in 1949) in 100 or 120 news items, consisting of 32,000 words of domestic and 30,000 words of foreign news.
2. To domestic provincial and municipal papers, 35,000 words per day, transmitted as was the previous category by the copying method—Chinese characters are written on a tape for facsimile transmission by machine, a method that obviates the ciphering and deciphering process—at 6,000 words per hour.

3. To small papers below the provincial level, about 10,000 words per day, comprising 6,000 words for city papers and 3,500 words for rural papers, sent through Hellschreiber and voicecast.
4. English broadcast at 3,000–12,000 words per day (2,000 words in 1949), in nine separate routes: by radioteletype to London, by Hellschreiber to Prague, Hong Kong, Tokyo, Karachi, and by Morse code to Southern Europe, Cairo, Puongyang, Hanoi and Yalta.
5. Russian broadcast of 8,000–10,000 words per day to the Tass news agency.

There is every reason to believe that the NCNA has expanded its operations during the last decade, although the volume of its output has yet to impress journalists in the United States. There is no need to speculate on how effectively the NCNA has served the Chinese Communists: If it is not very effective as a gatherer and distributor of news, it is at least efficient in centralizing the Party's control of news dissemination.

7. MASS COMMUNICATION: RADIO

One may find it difficult to believe that in China, where radio transmission and receiving facilities are few and inadequate, radio can be at all effective as a means of disseminating propaganda. But the vast land of China is now blanketed by a round-the-clock din of radio. As Sripati Chandra-sekhar, a noted Indian scholar who returned in 1959 from extensive travel behind the Bamboo Curtain, described it, the radio voice "blares away at one in the bus, in the train, in the tram, in Pullman sleepers and dining cars, on street corners, in villages, towns, and cities—just about everywhere." He goes on to say:

> Even in the most backward and traditional villages I saw the loudspeakers hidden in treetops. One can escape the sun and moon—but not the loudspeaker. . . .
> [This] is the most important mass medium for the official "news" —news of the nation's progress, the industrial output, instructions on how to make a native shelter, how to defeat the American "imperialist" and the Chiang clique, how to be a good Communist, how to be neat, how to denounce the rightist, how to cook sweet potatoes, where not to spit, and a thousand other things, interspersed with the traditional Chinese opera, with its deafening gongs and cymbals, as well as martial music and marching songs. A few times on the Pullman, I had to feign illness so that I could remove the plug under the loudspeaker in order to enjoy a few hours of quiet. The citizen does not have a minute of silence in which to rest his mind or reflect on his new life.[1]

Ever since 1949, in fact, the Communists have shrewdly and vigorously utilized radio as a major weapon of propaganda to facilitate their control of the nation. A radio set is, however, still something of a luxury in China. In June, 1950, an official announcement reported only eighty-three radio stations in the entire country—fifty-one government-owned stations and thirty-two privately-owned stations (twenty-two of the latter in Shanghai).[2] At about the same time, only 1–1.1 million "serviceable receiving sets" were reported, and most of them only in big cities like Shanghai, Canton, Nanking, and Hankow.[3] Although the regime undoubtedly has been trying to improve the broadcasting system, an announcement in 1956 still could boast of only 1.5 million regular receiving sets for a population of 600 million.[4]

The Chinese Communists have not been unaware of the seriousness of the problem—of insufficient radio facilities and limited resources available for broadcasting. Nevertheless, these technical handicaps have not prevented them from making radio a major propaganda weapon: Their solution to the problem is what is known as *kuang po shu ying wang,* or radio-receiving networks.

There are two distinctive features of these networks: The first is technical, what the Communists call *yu hsien kuang po,* or "line broadcasting." The networks are not, strictly speaking, broadcasting systems, but a system of point-to-point radio communication, with dissemination of selected programs at the point of reception by means of wired loudspeakers. (This is known as the "radio-diffusion exchange" system in the Soviet Union[5] or "community listening" in some other countries.) The operation is extremely simple. The system consists primarily of a transformer, a loudspeaker, a switch, and a volume control. Listeners hear the programs over wired speakers like those of a public-address system. These loudspeakers are generally located in dormitories, communal dwellings, and in public places such as recreation halls, town halls, and village centers. An operator—known as a monitor—can connect this speaker system with a receiver of either local or national programs. At any time, he may interrupt to make statements, in the form of announcements or "cultural" and "educational" material designed especially for his audience.

The second striking feature of the networks concerns the audience, and the technique the Communists call "collective listening." Most radio listeners are workers in factories and mines, peasants on farms, and people of low cultural standard in cities. These are "organized" and "mobilized" to form "radio-listening groups."

Trained monitors are located throughout the country to make certain that the daily messages from Peking find their way to the masses of people organized in these groups. They also see to it that certain messages requiring serious attention are discussed and understood in "political study groups."

This entire system of radio networks emerged almost immediately after the Communists conquered the mainland, when an important government document made clear that "the work of broadcasting must be developed."[6] It was followed by several directives from the Central People's Government and the Chinese Communist Party, which gave concrete instructions on how that development would take place. In April, 1950, the Press Association's Bureau of Broadcasting, which supervised broadcasting at that time, issued the "Decisions Regarding the Establishment of Radio-Receiving Networks."[7] In it, all government agencies, units of the People's Liberation Army, and mass organizations were asked to do their best to install transmitting stations and wired loudspeakers and to train monitors.

The emphasis at that point was on training the monitors. Their principal duties were to mobilize listeners in factories, villages, schools, institutions, or even streets; to pick up the daily news and comments, and central or local government directives and distribute them to local institutions or groups in the form of small-size newspapers, mimeographed sheets, blackboard newspapers, wall newspapers, or group meetings.

How successful the project was in 1950 is not clearly known, although the press frequently reported various kinds of "accomplishments." The receiving network in the southwest, for instance, was in an area where communications and press facilities were generally poor and the rate of illiteracy comparatively high. According to an official release, in the five provinces in this area, there were 259 receiving stations, not including those in Chengtu and Kweiyang. In north Szechuan alone, the Communists reported forty stations, of which twelve published mimeographed newspapers and twenty-three operated blackboard newspapers. It was estimated that the monitors were able to mobilize a daily audience of more than 1 million persons in the area.[8]

On September 12, 1951, another important directive was released, "Regarding the Establishment of Radio Broadcasting and Receiving Networks in all Factories, Mines and Enterprises in the Country," promulgated by the Press Administration and the All-China Federation of Labor Unions.

1. In all publicly-run factories, mines, and enterprises where there are 300 or more workers or staff members and where no wired speakers have been set up, the labor unions in the unit should cooperate with related administrative units to plan for the setting up of such a system. In those units where radio equipment is available, effort should be made for further development to make the full use of the service.

2. In the dormitories of all factories, mines, and enterprises, the administrative staff members, union officers, and representatives of workers' families should work together to organize radio-receiving groups so that all workers and their families can constantly receive political and cultural education. If conditions permit, wired speakers must be provided.

3. In those organizations where wired speakers are available, the main tasks are as follows: to organize various kinds of programs in harmony with the production, learning, and cultural-recreational activities of the organization; to complete the specially assigned tasks of the higher administrative authorities; and to relay programs concerning working people from the People's Broadcasting Station.

4. All radio-receiving stations in factories, mines, and enterprises must make periodic reports on their situations (such as the organizational structure of wired broadcasts and radio-receiving stations, responsible personnel, equipment, size of audience, etc.) and plans to the All-China Federation of Labor, Radio Broadcasting Bureau of the Press Administration, and the local people's broadcasting stations.

5. All labor unions in factories, mines and enterprises must consider radio-receiving and broadcasting as the major task of the departments handling cultural and educational affairs. They should constantly direct such activities and make full use of broadcasts to push forward the programs of production, to organize current affairs study groups, and to develop all political, educational, and cultural activities.[9]

Between 1951 and 1954, the Communist regime concentrated on the development of radio-relay stations and collective-listening groups in factories, mines, enterprises and the army. Although sporadic reports were made from time to time about broadcasting work in rural areas, it was only logical to start with whatever equipment was at hand. i.e.. in large cities where radio facilities were readily available. In 1955, however, Peking began to turn to the rural areas. On July 30, 1955, the National Conference of People's Representatives voted that, "By 1957, there should be 30,000 radio broadcasting and relay stations in the cities and villages."[10] It was also decided that broadcasting in areas of national minority groups should be developed.[11]

In December of the same year, the Third National Conference on Broadcasting Work was held in Peking to map plans for the "development of more than 900 line-broadcasting stations in the country in 1956, with a total of 450,000–500,000 wired loudspeakers, 80 per cent of which will be installed in the rural areas."[12] The NCNA further reported:

> By the end of 1957, there will be more than 1,800 broadcasting [relay] stations in the rural areas throughout the country, with 1,360,000 loudspeakers. In some provinces the situation will be reached where broadcasts will reach every *tsun* [village] and every cooperative. By 1962, there will be more than 5,400 line broadcasting stations in the rural areas of the whole country, with 6,700,000 loudspeakers.[13]

The policy on constructing the rural network, as set out by the Third National Conference on Broadcasting Work, called for: "Reliance on the masses; utilization of existing equipment; development by stages and gradual regularization of the network; first reaching the villages and the cooperatives, and later the homes of the peasants."[14] To persons unfamiliar with the Chinese language or with Communist expressions, the policy needs some explanation. "Reliance on the masses" actually means that the peasants were supposed to contribute actively to the project: "Reliance on the masses not only refers to the question of the construction cost, but after the broadcasting network has been built, the masses must further be relied upon for inspection, repairs, maintenance and management."[15] "Utilization of existing equipment," according to the Communists, "is in keeping with the practice of thrift and practicability, the promotion of the spirit of economy."[16] In practice, this means using existing telephone posts, cables, and buildings. "Development by stages," the Communists cautiously point out, "does not mean the spreading over many quarters or years the work which can be accomplished within a single quarter or a single year."[17]

One can readily see that the regime made no heavy financial investment in launching such a gigantic project. The people carried the major burden.

It is no simple coincidence, incidentally, that the development of broadcasting in rural areas took place after 1955. It came simultaneously with the promotion of "agricultural cooperatives," in full swing throughout China. And there were other "cultural" and "educational" projects to be either introduced or intensified among the peasants. Needless to say, the regime needed radio to transmit the messages of the government and Party to facilitate its various tasks:

> The line broadcasting system is regularly used for the political and cultural education of the peasants, the improvement of mass political work in the rural areas, the promotion of the political and production enthusiasm of the peasants, the extension of advanced experiences in agricultural production, and the enlivenment of the cultural life in the rural areas. The rural broadcasting network also plays a marked role in the forecasting of weather conditions for the protection of agricultural production.[18]

Up-to-date information regarding wired radio in rural areas is lacking, but the regime frequently reports the accomplishments of a "model" area or sometimes singles out other areas for criticism. One of these "models" is Chiu Tai, a town in the province of Kirin. According to *Jen Min Jih Pao*, the broadcasting project was formally begun there on April 1, 1952. By January, 1956, more than 90 per cent of the area was served by the radio-receiving network, consisting of two 500-watt transmitters, one 250-watt transmitter, 2,100 *li** of cable, 876 wired loudspeakers in the town, and 180 loudspeakers in surrounding areas. About 2,000 wired loudspeakers were to be installed in the spring of 1956, another 3,500 loudspeakers before the end of 1956, and 3,500 more in 1957.[19]

* Li is a Chinese measure of distance equal to about one-third of a mile.

In another issue of *Jen Min Jih Pao*, it was reported that the province of Kirin was to have 80,000 wired loudspeakers by 1957.[20]

But these stories of success, even if one does not question their accuracy, should not lead one to conclude that the radio propaganda system of China is flawless. A long article in *Kuang Min Jih Pao* complained in March, 1956:

> During the few months since the undertaking of the development of the rural broadcasting network . . . a good job has not been done in all areas, and in some localities many problems exist. . . . Some comrades fail to have a full understanding of the importance of reliance on the activeness of the masses . . . and there are reported instances of forced allocation of quotas.
>
> In some *hsien*, every cooperative in the area was called upon to pay its share of the contributions to such costs, with the result that after the payment was made, the loudspeakers were not installed and there was great dissatisfaction among the masses.
>
> In some areas, the branch wires reaching the cooperatives are simply tapped on the telephone wires. In some areas, most of the poles erected have already been blown down.[21]

Local Program Content

Early on in the development of radio-receiving networks, most relay stations paid most attention to the programs transmitted from the Central People's Broadcasting Station in Peking, or from regional and provincial stations. At least, this was the policy of the propaganda officials responsible for the networks in Chiu Tai, in Kirin: "To rebroadcast is the major task; to originate programs locally is a secondary duty."[22] However, at the Fourth National Conference of Broadcasters, held in July, 1956, in Peking, it was decided that, "While to relay certain programs of the Central People's Broadcasting Station at specified hours is necessary, a more important task should be to strive to improve locally-originated programs."[23]

A review of the news stories and editorials in the Chinese press reveals that the main purposes of radio-receiving networks in rural areas are: to promote higher productivity; to inform listeners on important current affairs; to explain important policies of the Party and the government; to report new scientific methods in agriculture; to fight against old, traditional and superstitious beliefs; to assist listeners in their political studies; to organize or mobilize them for specific tasks of the Party or government; and to publicize "cultural" activities. In rural areas, "cultural" activities mean projects of mass education.

The following policy on local programs set out by the propaganda authorities in Chiu Tai is typical:

> The major content of locally-originated programs should be: To publicize and promote agricultural cooperatives, to constantly stimulate the enthusiasm for labor among peasants; to agitate for high agricultural production, and to satisfy the peasants' demands for cultural life. All these should be done by making use of "model" or "progressive" activists and introducing their "progressive experience."[24]

The following are samples of specific programs: "Experience of Setting Up an Agricultural Co-op," "Village Correspondents," "Program in Ideology," "Reports on Production and Experience in Villages," "How Agricultural Mutual-Aid Teams Challenge Each Other in Production Races," "Directives, Announcements and Comments on Production Races," "Local Drama," and "Folk Music."[25]

How much or what specific kinds of programs are available from the Central People's Broadcasting Station in Peking or by regional and provincial stations cannot be exactly determined, but it is known that the Peking Station has special programs designed for and beamed to workers in factories, peasants in villages, or soldiers in the army.

The central themes of propaganda over the Home Service of the Peking Station are, however, simple enough: Work harder, produce more, donate more, love Communism, hate America and all other defined enemies within and without, trust the Party, and have faith in a bright future. In all their simplicity, these themes are repeated endlessly in a thousand ways, but always in a decisive, demanding and convincing tone and in practically every program that is broadcast, even in music or youth programs.[26]

In 1951, political propaganda on the Home Service of the Peking Station—news, commentaries, press reviews, news dictations, political talks and "cultural" programs—occupied more than 70 per cent of the program schedule.[27] And essentially the same was true of the programs of the East China People's Broadcasting Station in Shanghai.[28] In 1955, however, a Communist magazine reported that news and political broadcasts of the Central People's Broadcasting Station was reduced to about 30 per cent of the total broadcasting time, and that musical, literary, dramatic, "cultural" and scientific programs occupied about 60 per cent of the total time.[29]

One service provided by the Central People's Broadcasting Station especially for radio-receiving networks and "propagandists" is the program of news dictations.[30] In Chinese, this program is known as "*chi lu hsin wen*," which means "news to be recorded." It generally starts with a preview of the next day's news or features. Sometimes "special notes to propagandists and monitors" instruct the monitors and propagandists as to what issue and what angle they should play up. Then the announcer gives the topics of the items for dictation as well as the number of Chinese characters in each item. The speed of dictation is very slow, and every sentence is repeated at least three or four times so that the listener can easily take it down in longhand.

It is easy to understand why and how such service is of great propaganda value. First, it is a cheap way for the Party to reach a large number of people. A monitor requires no more than an ordinary radio to receive the messages, but if the messages were transmitted by a news agency through cable, a more expensive apparatus would have to be installed at every receiving point and more trained personnel would be needed. Secondly, since the Peking Station has sole control over information transmitted for national use, the Party can be assured of a high degree of conformity in the news made available. Thirdly, it is supposed to help the local propagandists, who would otherwise have to struggle to acquire and write material for their own local propaganda publications. (It should be remembered that many, if not most, of the propagandists and monitors are not persons of high cultural attainments.) It eliminates all problems of gathering and editing news, of censorship, and, above all, of interpretation of events which Peking alone is in a position to interpret "correctly." Finally, since the monitors are informed of programs ahead of time, it is easier for them to arrange local programs or to mobilize listeners.

It is difficult to assess the success or failure of radio propaganda in Communist China. But one thing appears to be certain: in the fourteen years since the Communists took over the mainland, they have tried hard to improve the effectiveness of this particular medium of mass persuasion and to make their radio propaganda more interesting and palatable to the listeners. The time devoted to straight, undiluted political propaganda programs has been gradually and consistently reduced, while more programs of music and entertainment have been introduced. This is not to suggest that the regime has relaxed its efforts in mass persuasion or that it has diluted its political propaganda. Apparently the Communist leaders have made these changes simply to "sugar-coat" their propaganda—an attempt to be somewhat subtler in their persuasion. These changes can be easily seen when one compares the radio programs of the leading stations during the early years of the regime with those of recent years.[31]

Take, for instance, the East China People's Broadcasting Station, which was established on April 1, 1950. On that day, the Shanghai *Ta Kung Pao* printed a complete broadcasting schedule of the station, whose programs were on the air for sixteen hours:

First Program

6:00 A.M.	Overture, announcements of the day's program
6:15	Russian lessons
7:00	News in Shanghai
7:30	Rebroadcast of Mandarin newscasts of the Central People's Broadcasting Station
7:45	News in East China
8:00	Intermission
9:00	Interest rates and quotations (not on Sundays)
9:05	Mandarin opera
9:25	Currency exchange quotations and retail rice prices (no program on Sundays)
10:00	News dictation from Peking station

Second Program

12:00 P.M.	Overture and announcements
12:15	Reviews of books and movies; news in publications
12:30	Rebroadcast of Mandarin Newscasts of the Central People's Broadcasting Station

12:45	Russian lessons
1:30	News in East China
1:45	Music
4:00	News dictation for East China
4:40	Business news in East China

Third Program

5:00 P.M.	Overture and announcements
5:10	Spoken drama and stories
6:00	Music lessons and teaching of singing (musical programs on Sundays)
6:45	Service for listeners (questions and answers)
7:00	Questions and answers in political study
7:15	News in East China
7:30	Correspondence from East China
7:45	Market news (music records on Sundays)
8:00	Rebroadcast of news, international news commentaries, speeches, and correspondence from the Central People's Broadcasting Station
9:00	Russian lessons
9:45	Business news (music records on Sundays)
10:00	Special broadcasts to Taiwan
11:00	Announcements of next day's programs

According to this schedule, news and news dictation occupied almost one-third of the total program schedule. Music and other entertainment programs were not given much time:

	Minutes	Percentage
News	220	22.76%
News dictation	120	12.45
Russian lessons	135	14.02
Announcements	45	4.67
Market news	90	9.33
Political talks	15	1.55
Music	155	16.02
Reviews of books and movies	15	1.55
Spoken drama and stories	50	5.19
Teaching of singing	45	4.67
Broadcasts to Taiwan	60	6.24
Others	15	1.55
TOTAL:	965	100.00

Two years later, in 1952, a broadcasting schedule of the Home Service of the central station in Peking appeared in the January 31, 1952, issue of the *Chang Chiang Jih Pao* (*Yangtze Daily,* Wuhan), the most important Party newspaper in Central-South China. According to this schedule, the Peking Home Service offered at this time three programs every day. The complete schedule is given as follows:

First Program

6:45 A.M.	National anthem
6:50	Physical exercise
6:55	Physical exercise
7:00	News
7:15	Physical exercise
7:20	Lectures on physical exercise
7:40	Physical exercise
7:45	Music
8:00	News
8:15	News dictation

Second Program

11:55 A.M.	National anthem
12:00 P.M.	Peking opera
12:30	News
12:45	Army program: Overture: "Song of three disciplines and eight attentions" (No program on Saturday)
1:15–2:15	News dictation for armed forces (No program on Saturday)

Third Program

5:25 P.M.	National anthem
5:30	Program for children and youth: Overture: "Song of the youth corps"
6:00	Army program: Overture: "Song of the three disciplines and eight attentions"
6:30	Literary and art program
7:00	Economic news ("Literary and art programs" on Saturday)
7:30	Cultural program ("Literary and art programs" on Saturday; 6:30–8:00 P.M., "Saturday soiree on literature and art")

8:00	Joint program of the people's broadcasting stations in the country
8:30	International news
8:45	Literary and art program
9:30	News
9:45	News dictation

As one can readily see, political propaganda dominated the Home Service's program schedule. But the Chinese Communists were shrewd enough not to follow too long this plan for radio propaganda. In 1954–55, they began to make rather elaborate changes: Their special kind of "radio drama" had already become a form of popular art, so they particularly emphasized it, and urged the stations to make their other programs more attractive.

More and more music programs of various kinds were also added. By 1958–59, music had become a major ingredient in Chinese broadcasting. The regular features of Mandarin or Peking opera and of folk music were particularly popular. The Chinese Communists have done much to revive and popularize folk music; they have been quite successful in using popular art forms for propaganda, and few folk-music programs are entirely free from political propaganda.

One needs only a quick glance at the following program of the Peking Broadcasting Station (a local station, *not* the Central People's Broadcasting Station in Peking) on August 17, 1959, to discover the changes in Chinese Communist broadcasting that occurred after 1955.

5:55 A.M.	Sign-on: Overture, preview of program
6:00	Tsou-chow music [a kind of folk music]
6:15	Weather for Peking area
6:30	Music: Symphonic music by Czech composers
6:45	Weather for Peking area and News
7:00	Voice recital by members of the Central Music Corps: "Yellow River Song"; "Song of Water-barrow"; "Oh Horse, Run Fast"; "Now Our Songs are Measured by Bushels"; "Song of Peacock"; "Song of October Revolution"; "Cowboy Songs"; "Song of Fisherwoman"; and "Mama, I Want To Go to the Countryside"
7:30	Weather for Peking area and Life in the Capital
8:00	Children's calisthenics program

8:10	Summertime story-telling program for children
8:40	Music: folk songs of Albania
9:00	Intermission
10:00	Calisthenics
11:25	Overture, program preview
11:30	Music: Mongolian instrumental music
11:45	Music: Hungarian music
12:00 P.M.	Weather
12:15	News
12:30	Broadcasts to suburbs and rural areas
1:00	Serial novel: "Military Workers Corps Behind Enemy Lines"
1:30	Music: Folk music of Chin region
2:00	Intermission
3:00	Music recital: "Oh, What a Beautiful Mountain and River View!"; "Return to Mother's House"; "Shepherd's Evening Song"; "Autumn Harvest"; "Song of Postmen"; "Song of Cooking Staff"; and Mongolian songs
3:40	Music
4:10	Music: Beethoven and others
4:30	Calisthenics
4:40	Light music: Czech performing group
5:00	Peking opera
5:30	Program of cultural recreation
5:45	Weather
6:00	Music: Hopei folk music
6:30	Broadcasts to youth and children
7:00	News
7:15	Broadcasts to school-age children
7:30	Music: Western and brass music
7:45	Weather and Life in the Capital
8:15	Music: folk music of northern Shansi
8:30	Rebroadcast of programs by regional stations
9:00	Broadcasts to suburbs and rural areas
9:30	Music: Chinese-violin solo [a kind of two-string instrument]
9:45	News
10:45	Music: folk music
10:30	Peking regional drama
12:00 A.M.	Sign-off[32]

8. *MASS COMMUNICATION:* TATZEPAO (POSTERS)

Tatzepao is a new term coined by the Chinese Communists, which literally means a "paper of big letters or bold characters." (The closest English translation is "poster" or "placard.") It is simply a large sheet of paper posted at any convenient location for people to read. It is hand-written and does not have any particular format or style. It is an unusually powerful weapon of persuasion which has been perfected, though not invented, by Communist propagandists.

That posters are used for propaganda purposes is hardly unusual; that they should be used as a medium of "mass communication" is something strikingly new. The very fact that posters have to be hand-written would seem to preclude their use for a mass audience. Nevertheless, *tatzepao*, first used on a dramatically large scale during the "Hundred Flowers" or Rectification Movement in 1957, is now regarded as the "most effective medium for criticism and self-criticism."[1] In 1960, when the Movement to Increase Production and Practice Austerity was in full swing, *tatzepao* was considered a major weapon of indoctrination.[2] According to Mao, "*tatzepao* is, under the present conditions, the best form of *tou cheng*, which is beneficial to the proletariat but damaging to the bourgeois."[3]

> It is good to use *tatzepao* in our rectification campaign in factories. The more we use, the better. If you have 10,000 sheets of *tatzepao* in your plant, that is first class. If you have 5,000 sheets, that is second class. 2,000 sheets means third class. If you have only a few scattered sheets here and there, then you don't count at all.[4]

The following is a vivid description of the use of *tatzepao* on a university campus. It is an eyewitness report by Max Snurderl, professor of law at Ljubljana University in Yugoslavia and a member of the Yugoslav National Assembly, who visited Peking in 1958.

At the National University of Peking, the Yugoslav visitor was told that "the students there had twice broken the record for writing posters in 1957 and 1958," and that "they had recently drawn 500,000 posters attacking waste and intolerance."

> All the walls of the numerous buildings of the university, inside and out, were hung with posters as high as a man could reach! In front of the buildings, there were racks on which posters hung. Every corridor was decorated with posters. Strings were stretched across the corridors from one wall to the other, with posters hanging from them like laundry hung to dry. You had to stoop in order to pass under them as you walked along the corridors.
>
> I thought this was only a specialty of the National University. Soon I found that the making of posters had become the first and foremost method of general education and political indoctrination. . . .
>
> I found the flood of posters at every university, faculty, high school, and institution I visited in Peiping, Shanghai, Nanking and Wuchang. I was told that such posters could also be found in offices, hospitals, and elsewhere.[5]

It is not surprising that the Yugoslav visitor was both fascinated and terrified by the extensive use of *tatzepao* for political indoctrination. For at no time in the entire course of Chinese history—indeed in the history of any nation in the world—has such a medium of communication been so widely used and shrewdly manipulated. The following are typical cases that illustrate this form of mass persuasion.

A. Chung Min, member of the Shanghai Municipal Committee of the Chinese Communist Party, reported in 1958:

> During this anti-extravagance and anti-conservatism movement, the broad masses and cadres in Shanghai have produced in the period slightly more than 100 million sheets of *tatzepao*. . . .
>
> The Shipbuilding Yard posted 538,000 sheets of *tatzepao* in a short period of six or seven days.

Experience has told us: jointly used with discussion meetings, accusation meetings and debate sessions, *tatzepao* is the most effective method to bare and solve the problem of internal contradiction among the people. . . .

Tatzepao is a driving force to enable us to accomplish our tasks. It is a form of pressure to those cadres who are at a low level of class consciousness . . .

Tatzepao is something unique in our country of socialist democracy. It is the best instrument to bring to the open the problem of internal contradiction among the people, to solve the problem and thus to push forward progress. We should follow Comrade Mao's direction to develop and keep this particular instrument and to keep it forever.[6]

B. In November, 1957, a total of 220 sheets of *tatzepao* were posted by some 60 units of government offices in Peking, along with 1,400 meetings. "Through these channels, the masses contributed some 380,000 items of suggestions."[7]

C. Wan Ching-liang, the First Secretary of the Party Committee of Patung, a small city near Shanghai, opened his article "Long Live the Commune" with these words:

After the news about the people's communes appeared in newspapers last year, the broad masses of peasants in Patung welcomed the idea enthusiastically and demanded speedy establishment of the commune. When the authorities decided to have the commune established, the masses posted more than 30,000 sheets of *tatzepao* in a few days resolutely asking to join the people's commune.[8]

D. One New China News Agency reporter describes:

There are now so many *tatzepao* in the government agencies that sharply colored "no smoking" signs have to be put up. Indeed *tatzepao* are plentiful. You see them from one floor to another, on all walls, on windows, at staircases and inside of offices. In corridors, strings or ropes were stretched from one wall to another to hang the reams and reams of *tatzepao*.[9]

In some quarters, the production of *tatzepao* has become a formalized affair run almost like a newspaper, complete with "editorial board, production center, correspondent network and distribution center."[10] In others, for those who cannot write, special *"tatzepao* writing stations" are established.[11]

There is no set form or style for *tatzepao*. It appears with slogans, satirical prose, comic strips, cartoons, accusation letters, tables, graphs, and songs. While most *tatzepao* are hand-written papers posted on the wall, many are produced on blackboards, and it is not uncommon for *tatzepao* to be written with chalk on any kind of surface, including cement or wooden floors. Some *tatzepao* are so large that they cover several walls; others show simple slogans of a few Chinese characters. In one magazine, a Communist writer was praised for producing 100 *tatzepao* in three nights without sleep. He produced forty sheets during the first night, twenty-five the following night, and the rest the third. Apparently exhausted after three sleepless nights, his 100th *tatzepao* consisted only of two slogans with ten Chinese characters: *"Kung Tsang Tang Wan Sui! Mao Tsu Hsi Wan Sui!"* ("Long Live the Communist Party! Long Live Chairman Mao!")[12]

But not many *tatzepao* merely parrot such popular (though vague and ritualistic) slogans. Most of them have something specific to say and are often addressed to a particular group or individual. The following *tatzepao*, written by Yang Su-ying, a tenth-grader in the Third Girls School in Peking, for instance, was addressed to her teacher, Tsou Ching-san, who was severely though politely criticized for the way his history class was handled:

> Your lectures are very systematic. This is not to be denied. But history is a science which is ideologically important and politically potent, and all problems in history should be analyzed from the class viewpoint. It seems to me that you, sir, have not done so. You do not distinguish what should be loved and what should be hated.
>
> For instance, you always have supplementary material or data for your lectures. But such materials are generally relevant to conditions in palaces or lives of emperors and those who represent the bourgeois class. You don't engage in criticism of such things. But when you come to the part on the October Revolution, you supply no supplementary material. You merely repeat what is written in the textbook. And you have no analysis either.
>
> This is bad, if we measure your performance against the standard

of the "teachers of the people" or "proletarian teachers" who should be both Red and expert.

When you lectured on Napoleon, you described him as a man who was a genius in organization and military affairs. You even went into the minute details of his personal appearance—how short he was or how much taller his aides were, etc. But when you came to the lecture on the awakening of Asia, you merely dismissed the revolutionary movements in various countries in a very casual manner. You didn't carefully discuss all these revolutionaries. Why do you pay so much attention in your lectures to those reactionary characters in history? And why do you treat so lightly and casually the great revolutions in history?[13]

Another girl in the same school wrote an even longer *tatzepao* accusing her composition teacher of being "ideologically questionable" because of the way he graded papers and wrote comments. She cited specific comments on her papers to suggest her teacher's "reactionary" and unfavorable attitude toward the Party and the new society. While these letters were quite severe, the girls were careful enough to observe the traditional rules of etiquette and courtesy when addressing teachers. (For instance, the polite expression for the word 'you' was used throughout.) There was harshness in the criticism, but no rudeness in the manner.

That *tatzepao* should be unusually effective as a means of persuasive communications is easy to understand. In the first place, it is written by and about people whom all the readers know. In the second place, it cannot be ignored or dismissed, for it may appear on the wall of one's office or at the door of one's house. (This happened in one case of an engineer who was accused of having committed the unforgivable sin of "individualism." *Tatzepao* appeared in his office. As a matter of self-defense, he wrote his own, entitled "My Difficulties." But his *tatzepao* got nowhere; it only invited more *tatzepao* from his accusers. According to the Communist news story, the engineer, after the "repeated education" of the *tatzepao*, realized his mistakes, and in his later *tatzepao*, accepted the criticisms, writing many more to "expose" the various aspects of "extravagance," "waste," and "undesirable behavior" in his plant.[14])

As a device for political indoctrination and thought reform, *tatzepao* is, in fact, in some respects far more effective than the newspaper columns of criticism and self-criticism. To begin with, it is physically impossible for a newspaper to involve all its readers directly in criticism and self-criticism. It can only print a limited number of stories attacking an individual or groups, and there is no guarantee that all its readers will be equally interested in all the cases. But virtually everyone in China is within the reach of a *tatzepao*. Its ideological assault is at once personal and direct, and the accused must react not only correctly but also immediately. Almost everyone in Communist China today is in one way or another involved in this particular form of persuasion.

Peking has done an enormous amount of work to turn this common, crude, and inexpensive form of communication into a widely used and tightly controlled tool of mass persuasion. How a Party member is expected to use this particular political weapon is vividly described in the following poem, which appeared in a special Communist poetry magazine:

All lights are out;
All people are sound asleep.
But who is still writing *tatzepao?*
Oh, yes! It is our Party Secretary.

He integrates the wisdom of the masses;
He records all the wishes of the people.
All the sincere feelings and true sentiments
Sometimes make him excited, sometimes make him wonder.

He gazes at his *tatzepao,*
Like the way a soldier gazes at a trench.
A fighting plan is already born in his mind;
A blue-print for his work tomorrow is drawn.

It is now late in the night,
And all is quiet.
His silver hair waves in the breeze;
From his pen one hears sa, sa, sa, . . .[15]

9. MASS COMMUNICATION: FILM

The mission of China's film industry, according to Hsia Yen, Vice Minister of Cultural Affairs and China's leading spokesman on motion pictures, "is to reflect speedily the new era and new society —especially the new men, new events, new heroes, new ideologies, new emotions, new morality, and new qualities during this period of socialist revolution and socialist development—and through all this to propagate the Socialist and Communist ideology."[1]

The Chinese Communist regime has made every effort to expand the film industry and to give the movie screen a prescribed and wide-ranging political function. It has proudly and frequently reported, therefore, that motion pictures are reaching a much larger audience than before in the country. For instance, the figure for mobile projection teams, according to Hsia, "jumped from about 600 in 1949 to about 14,500 by the end of 1959.[2] The movie audience, estimated at 50 million in 1949 by another Communist source, reportedly rose to 1.39 billion in 1956.[3] Even as early as 1954, the Communists claimed that their "cinema production teams serving mines, factories, villages and settlements in mountainous and remote frontier districts of the country gave more than 1.1 million shows to a total audience of 820 million people."[4]

Such figures may not be fabricated or exaggerated, although Communist statistics are often inflated and rarely reliable, for the film has become a part of the grand scheme of mass persuasion and the regime is quite adept at "mobilizing" the movie audience. Consider, for instance, the following case.

In December, 1951, in the midst of the Korean war, the Peking

Film Studio of the Ministry of Cultural Affairs released the first part of a documentary film called "Resist-America Aid-Korea." It was obvious that the Communists were eager to have a huge audience for this film, but they did not go about winning it simply by placing attractive advertisements in newspapers or on colorful posters on streets. Instead, a special committee was formed in every major city to see to it that the film was shown to the largest possible number of people. In Canton, "The Committee for Showing the Documentary Film, 'Resist-America Aid-Korea' " was formed of representatives of the 12 government and mass organizations: the Kwangtung Provincial Branch of the Resist-America Aid-Korea Association; Canton Municipal Branch of the Resist-America Aid-Korea Association; Commission of Cultural and Educational Affairs of the Kwangtung People's Government; Bureau of Civic Affairs of the Canton Municipal People's Government; Preparatory Committee of the Federation of Labor in Canton; Canton Branch of the New Democratic Youth Corps; Preparatory Committee of the Canton Democratic Women's Federation; Canton Federation of Students; Preparatory Committee of the Canton Educational Workers' Union; Canton Branch of the Sino-Soviet Friendship Association; and the South China Branch Office of the China Film Company. The committee issued the following joint directive:

In accordance with the directive of the Central-South District Branch of the Resist-America Aid-Korea Association, we should do our best to assist the South China Branch of the China Film Company in showing Part I of the documentary film "Resist-America Aid-Korea" and to fight for the completion of the task of mobilizing an audience of 450,000 in Canton. . . .

This film is to be shown in all theaters in the city beginning the 28th of this month. It is expected that all related organizations, immediately after receiving this directive, will start informing the masses of people of their jurisdiction to organize and mobilize group audiences. It is also expected that all organizations will report the size of audiences to be mobilized and other related comments to this office and keep in touch with this office by phone every day so as to guarantee that this task of propaganda and donation will be achieved.[5]

According to the official *Nan Fang Jih Pao*, by December 25, 1951, an estimated audience of 525,000 was already reported to the committee. The quota of 450,000 was thus easily met in a few days, and nineteen theaters in Canton sold out 250 shows before the film opened on December 28.[6]

This particular documentary film, it must be noted, was not designed to give the audience the thrill of a war movie. It was shown at a time when practically everyone in China was a member of the Resist-America Aid-Korea Association and when the anti-American theme was present in virtually every mass movement. After seeing the movie, the people were to participate in discussion groups, in order to shake off their "Respect-America, Worship-America, and Love-America" mentality and to establish their "Despise-America, Condemn-America and Hate-America" viewpoint. In the meantime, they were to take an active role in Resist-America Aid-Korea activities—joining demonstration parades, "volunteering" to go to the Korea front, or "contributing" money to buy airplanes, tanks, and munitions.

But these statistics and examples by no means suggest or imply that the film has been an effective means of persuasive communication. The truth of the matter is that the Chinese Communists have encountered great difficulty in developing the film as a weapon of propaganda to serve the needs of the Party. Their record, in fact, has not been at all impressive.

Part of the difficulty can be attributed to film and equipment shortages, clearly illustrated by the limited number of feature films produced in China. Even in 1954, when a Communist official reported on the "growing film industry in China," he could list only ten feature films.[7]

But most of the regime's difficulty has been ideological rather than economic. Ironically, the Communist leaders, supposedly shrewd manipulators of persuasive propaganda, have yet to win the confidence and genuine support of workers in the movie industry. The fierce battles waged against the "rightist" film workers in 1957–58 may have silenced the "dangerous" or "anti-Party" criticisms, but they did not result in any positive or productive gains. Indeed, the irony is even greater: Many of the actors, writers, and producers who now appear to be disillusioned by the

Party had been its faithful members and ardent supporters long before 1949.

The history of the Chinese Communist use of film as a political weapon goes back to the early 1930's, when Communist artists and writers infiltrated the film industry in Shanghai and soon expanded their control over the industry as a whole. Their underground activities then, once vehemently denied in Yenan, are now hailed in Peking.[8] In those early days of China's film industry, Communist artists and writers helped the Party by controlling both the script-writing departments of major studios and the writing and editing of movie-review sections of newspapers, by planting "aggressive elements" in the industry, and by introducing Soviet films to China. Through them, many of the major themes of Marxist doctrine found their way to the screen, and through them, the Party was able to expose "undesirable" aspects of the Kuomintang and the old society—thus heightening people's hostility toward the Nationalist Government. And through them, the Party was able to discover, cultivate, and unite potential revolutionaries among the intellectuals.

Understandably, when the Peking regime was established in 1949, these artists and writers felt that their ideological dependability was beyond doubt and that the correctness of their political judgment had already been tested. Many of them found the rigid Party control of the screen industry at first irritable and then intolerable. Their first shock came when the Party took action on *The Life of Wu Hsun*, a feature film produced in 1951 by some of the Party's best artists. At first, it was warmly received and highly praised. Then suddenly it was condemned—a condemnation extended into a nation-wide campaign against the "bourgeois mentality" of writers and producers. *The Life of Wu Hsun* portrayed a famous beggar who begged for money to set up schools for poor children. It was severely criticized on the grounds that begging, even for such noble reasons, is undignified behavior that insults labor, and that the whole film vulgarized Marxist ideology. Moreover, the Party considered Wu a hypocrite and a man who worshipped and respected the rich man.

The Party's action puzzled the writers, producers, directors, and actors and for a while hardly anyone knew which was the correct Party line to follow. A long debate ensued in the press and in indoctrination sessions. Many artists and writers dutifully wrote confessions of their "mistakes," but few seemed to know what "correct" films they should write or produce. At any rate, very few feature films were turned out following the incident, and almost all that were dealt with one of the following themes: the leading role of the Chinese Communist Party; the glorious accomplishments of the guerrillas in wartime and of the People's Liberation Army; model workers in production; and the struggle against "feudalism" and "reactionary oppression." The themes were, of course, in line with the Party decree that the film industry must "concentrate all its energies on producing films of significance to all the masses of the people, dealing with their life, thoughts, and age-long strivings, with the insight of a developed revolutionary artistic vision."[9] But, judging by Communist reports during the "Hundred Flowers" campaign in 1957–58, the Party's "wisdom" in choosing to devote all its screen efforts exclusively to these themes was simply not "commonly understood" by many film workers.

A quick review of Chinese Communist comment in 1961 and 1962 on the motion picture reveals that the Party has yet to clear up all the ideological confusion. Apparently, the belief in "movies for movies' sake" or in "art for art's sake" is still held by some film workers. That such "erroneous belief" has been so frequently and vehemently attacked suggests its continued existence.

One is under the impression that Peking has attached far more importance to the development of mobile projection teams and to documentary, educational, art, and news films than to feature films. Perhaps they are more useful; perhaps there are only limited resources for only a small number of feature films each year; perhaps Peking is still searching for a way to solve the ideological problems among film workers. But one thing is clear: Peking has not been overwhelmingly successful in its use of the motion picture as a means of political propaganda.

10. *MASS COMMUNICATION: ART AND LITERATURE*

No discussion on persuasive communication in Communist China can be complete without reference to the various forms of art and literature: drama, opera, songs, novels, propaganda paintings (*hsien chuan hua*), street-corner shows (*kai tou chu*), comics, cartoons, etc. Early in 1942, when the Communists were still a minority group at Yenan, Mao wrote:

> The literature and art of the proletariat are part of the revolutionary program of the proletariat. As Lenin pointed out, they are "a screw in the machine." . . . Although literature and art are subordinate to politics, they in turn exert a tremendous influence upon politics. . . . They are like the aforementioned screws. They may be of greater or lesser importance, or primary and secondary value when compared with other parts of the machine; but they are nevertheless indispensable to the machine; they are indispensable parts of the revolutionary movement. If we had no literature and art, even of the most general kind, we should not be able to carry on the revolution or to achieve victory. It would be a mistake not to recognize this fact.[1]

Lu Ting-i, the Party's propaganda chief, echoed Mao in 1950: "Literature and art have always occupied an extremely important position in the revolutionary work of the Chinese people. The Chinese people consider art and literature as a major weapon for use in ideological education and struggle."[2]

Mao's and Lu's remarks serve to explain the importance that Chinese Marxists attach to the establishment of a special government agency to give "constant direction and correct guidance" to all literary and art activities in China. That agency is the Min-

148

istry of Cultural Affairs, which includes such units as the Bureau of Art, the Bureau of Cinematographic Art, the Bureau of Drama Reformation, the Bureau of Public Cultural Relations, the Central Music Conservatory, the Central Drama College, the Central Art College, and many other institutions.

At the first All-China Conference of Writers and Artists in July, 1949, the policy for literary and art movements was laid down, in the same direction that Mao pointed out earlier in his address to the Yenan Literary Meeting on May 2, 1942—the guiding principle being that literature and art should serve the interests of workers, peasants, and soldiers. Mao had emphasized that "Our literature and art . . . are intended primarily for the workers, peasants and soldiers, and only secondarily for the petty bourgeoisie," and that "therefore, we must propagandize only the ideology of workers, peasants and soldiers."

All culture and all present-day literature and art belong to a certain class, to a certain party, or to a certain party line. There is no such thing as art for art's sake, or literature and art that lie above class distinction or above partisan interests. There is no such thing as literature or art running parallel to politics or being independent of politics. . . .

We demand unity between politics and art; we demand harmony between content and form—the perfect blending of revolutionary political content with the highest possible level of artistic form.[3]

To be sure that this policy would be carried out successfully the Communists required all artists and writers henceforth to "identify themselves with the workers and peasants, labor and write among them, and learn from them." This means that artists and writers, as noted earlier, can no longer work "in private" even when agreeing to gear their work to the "glorious wisdom" of peasants and workers. They must be with the peasants and workers. As the Vice Minister of Cultural Affairs, Chou Yang, decreed: "It is of the utmost importance for a writer to maintain the closest contacts with the life and struggle of the great mass of the people. Only thus can he acquire a feeling for the new and the fresh and develop broad vision."[4] It is, therefore, no coincidence that thousands of artists and writers often find themselves toiling together with peasants and workers in the countryside and in factories, a situation considered one of the most important requirements of their work. Tien Han, one of China's leading playwrights, describes it thus: "Ever since the Hundred Flowers Rectification Campaign in 1957, teams of dramatic workers have gone to the mountains, to farms, to factories, to armies, to the front, to be intimately associated with workers, peasants, and soldiers. On the one hand, they participate in the labor of production; on the other, they perform for them."[5]

The Communist single-minded use of art and literature as a tool of political communication necessarily introduces into the substance of art new characters, new symbols, new images, new expressions, new forms. *The Folk Songs of the Great Leap Forward,* for instance, opens with the following poem (profusely praised by Chou Yang):

> We measure songs in bushels now;
> The thousand bushels fill a barn;
> Don't laugh if we use homely speech—
> Out in the fields it turns to grain.
>
> You need a proper hoe to farm,
> You need a proper voice to sing;
> Each one of us is a singer now—
> We'll sing till the Yangtze flows upstream.[6]

This may well be a fairly accurate example of the mass-produced song or poem. For, as Chou goes on to say, "They [songs and poems] have become a mode of political agitation in factories and farms. Weapons in the struggle to increase output, and the creation of the laboring people themselves, they are at the same time works of art the people can appreciate."

"Poetry is now integrated with work, while work has become poetry," say the Chinese Communists. Even such work as collecting manure can be expressed in poetry "both lyrical and picturesque," Chou says:

> The little boat loaded with dung
> Has frightened the moorhens away,

> Has shattered the stars in the stream
> In smoke that is misty and gray.
>
> The little boat loaded with dung,
> Its sculls creaking merrily still,
> Is passing the willow-clad shore
> To melt into Peach Blossom Hill.[7]

But the one over-riding theme in all songs and poems concerns the dignity and power of labor, and, above all, praise of the Party:

> We work at such white heat
> If we bump the sky it will break,
> If we kick the earth it will crack;
> Seas can be tamed,
> Great Mountains moved;
> If the sky falls, our co-op will mend it,
> If the earth splits, our co-op will patch it.
> With the Party to lead us,
> There's nothing we can't achieve.[8]
>
> Hey, Sun!
> Dare you take us on?
> We're at work for hours
> While you're still snug abed;
>
> We grope our way home in the dark
> Long after you down your tools to hide your head.
>
> Hey, sun!
> Dare you take us on?[9]
>
> If our leaders hold the ladder
> Then we can scale the sky;
>
> If our leaders drive into the sea
> Then we can capture dragons where they lie;
>
> If our leaders can move mountains,
> Then we can fill in seas and make them dry.[10]

New images emerge in love songs, which must now always be related to agricultural or industrial labor and production:

> He carries earth as swiftly as the wind.
> And with her load, she follows close behind.
> "Though past the fleecy clouds you fly away
> I mean to catch you up, cost what it may."[11]

As for the theater, it is perhaps the only form of mass culture that is widely popular in China's rural areas, and almost the only art in which Chinese peasants can participate in the higher form of China's traditional culture. A great variety of dramatic theater exists in China and every region has its own operatic, theatrical, or musical form. Almost every village has a space that can be used as its theater (sometimes located in a temple or an ancestral shrine or on the local fair grounds), where performances are given by local or traveling drama troupes.

The Communists are obviously aware of the particular possibilities of drama as a means of persuasive communication, and they have attached special importance to this form of propaganda. The number of dramatic artists and performers in China in 1949 was, according to the Communists, 50,900; it jumped to 260,000 in 1959. The regime now claims to have 39,000 workers' after-work performing troupes, and 244,000 agricultural after-work drama teams and cultural-workers' corps.[12]

In addition to reviving the traditional drama of China, the Chinese Communist regime has introduced many new forms of dramatic art for the purpose of political propaganda. Radio drama, for instance, is now hailed as "the light brigade in propagandizing the Party's policies."[13] Then there are street-corner shows, which are called "living newspapers." Even only one year after the establishment of the regime, *People's China* reported:

Every day during the last few days [late in 1950] in Peking alone, more than 5,000 players from schools, institutions, and dramatic clubs have given various street-corner shows. Among the most effective "living newspaper" plays are *Truman Dreams of Hitler* and *Dances of the Devils*—the devils being Truman, MacArthur, Chiang Kai-shek and many others.

Through the countryside of Hopei Province, 9,000 locally organized amateur troupes are traveling from village to village to give performances for the peasants in the long winter evenings. Around the theme of "protect the homeland," their plays are woven out of the stuff of their own experiences. Their true-life stories impress the audiences profoundly and often at the end of the show, the onlookers themselves join the players in shouting slogans. Many enroll immediately as volunteers for Korea on the spot.[14]

In 1958, when a coup d'etat in Iraq resulted in the overthrow of King Feisal's regime, the propaganda team of the All-China Playwrights Association lost no time in producing a "living newspaper" play called *The Result of a Traitor,* ridiculing the Iraqi premier's failure in his attempt to flee the country disguised as a woman.[15]

These plays may sound crude and unsophisticated, but many of them are written by China's leading writers. *Ah, Ya, Ya, Small American Moon,* which ridicules the smallness of American satellites, was written by four leading playwrights, including Chen Pai-cheng. *High-Class Garbage,* which attacks the "rightists" in the "Hundred Flowers" campaign, is the work of Liu Chang-len, another noted playwright.[16]

The manipulation of drama for persuasive purposes is so important that a current policy of the Peking regime is "to integrate dramatic arts with teaching in communes" and "to establish fine-arts schools" in all basic units of the communes.[17]

11. CONCLUSIONS

What is the impact of the Chinese Communist system of persuasive and coercive communications? How effective is it? What are the successes and failures of Chinese Communist propaganda? To what extent has the regime reshaped the thinking of the nation? What difficulties does it have? And what are its plans for the future?

These are troubling questions, to answer which in any detail goes beyond the scope of the present study. But some suggestions may be in order.

Experts on international affairs and on communications research have long been fascinated and disturbed by the Chinese variant of mass persuasion. Some are seriously skeptical of the power of Peking's grand propaganda scheme, and consider it too quaint to be effective. They stubbornly refuse to believe that any one party or regime can even hope to "remold" the thinking of almost one-quarter of the human race, even though this is the openly stated goal of Peking. Then there are scholars at the other extreme, whom the stories about brainwashing in Communist China leave spellbound. To them, the Chinese Communists are master persuaders with an incredible ability, as one writer puts it, "to penetrate into the consciences of men" and "to possess the Chinese population."

Both sets of observations are obviously wrong, if easily understandable. To be realistic, one must recognize the seriousness of Peking's commitment to propaganda as "the tradition of the Party" as "the fundamental working method," and at the same time realize the limitations of any propaganda, Communist or otherwise. Mass persuasion in Communist China is neither a conventional political trick nor a new kind of black magic. It is an instrument of

154

power, or a method of control, that has been carefully designed and vigorously utilized to mobilize the population to attain specially prescribed goals and to accept Communist doctrine; to disseminate new ideas; to eradicate hostile ideologies; to mold patterns of motivation; and to maximize the influence of the Party. It is not a sporadic or short-term affair; it is a permanent institution of social control.

The Chinese Communists did not actually invent this communications system. The technical difference between the Moscow and Peking propaganda systems is much smaller than is generally assumed; the Chinese originality lies in the intensity, scope, and skill of their propaganda-agitation, not in its philosophy or nature. That is to say, what is remarkable is that the Chinese Communists have managed to manipulate and control almost all forms of human communication. Specifically, they have succeeded, to the surprise of many observers, in integrating all oral, informal, casual, and traditional means of communication with the more conventional channels and methods of mass propaganda and indoctrination.

There is no doubt that Peking's propaganda-communications system is both pervasive and penetrating. Employing many crude but effective methods, and emphasizing personal contact between the masses and Party cadres, the Communists have succeeded in bringing more people into direct and close contact with the central government than ever before in Chinese history. It is no exaggeration to say that not a living soul in China today can possibly escape the far-reaching arms of the Party's propaganda apparatus.

Even if the system is not so successful in the positive aim of producing the particular thoughts and attitudes desired by the Party, it is at least reasonably effective in the negative aim of keeping out information and ideas that might weaken the Party's control. Screening all information that will reach the people, it makes any free exchange of ideas among men almost impossible.

The communications system also provides the Party with a continuous flow of information on the sentiments of the people and the country's psychological climate. This obviously puts the Communist rulers in an incontestably powerful position. Moreover, the system is backed by force, and, should persuasion fail, the regime does not hesitate to resort to violence, which, incidentally, should also be considered a means of communication. This has been repeatedly demonstrated in various stages of the Chinese Communist revolution. The coercive aspect of Chinese Communist rule leaves the population with no alternative but to accept the Party line, however reluctant they may be to do so.

But in evaluating Peking's mass persuasion, one must keep in mind that such strength in persuasion can be weakness at the same time. Consider the simple matter of repetition. For almost fifteen years, the Chinese people have been forced to listen to their Marxist rulers' ideas and views—over and over again, through all the different media, the same message presented in endlessly varied ways. One can, of course, argue that the more frequently an idea is repeated, the more likely it is to be perceived, remembered, and constantly reinforced. Hitler, a shrewd propagandist, apparently believed so when he wrote in *Mein Kampf:* "The intelligence of the masses is small, their forgetfulness is great. Effective propaganda must be confined to merely a few issues which can be easily assimilated. Since the masses are slow to comprehend, they must be told the same thing a thousand times." On the other hand, it is obvious that this day-in and day-out repetition, which can easily invite boredom and apathy, may be self-defeating, a weakness as well as a strength in mass persuasion.

Communist China's massive propaganda machine is periodically tightened up and geared to a higher speed of performance. Does this imply that the regime is constantly improving the efficiency of its propaganda machine? Or does it suggest that the masses lose enthusiasm for the Communist program, and the Party periodically realizes its need for a more effective and more elaborate propaganda plan and machine to regain the support of the population? For there is no doubt that the Chinese people are over-propagandized and over-agitated. Even if they are not disgusted or infuriated by the incessant propaganda and never-ending exhortations, many, if not most, of them become so exhausted by this barrage of words that their potential for serving the country has been in some fashion impaired. They may react, and they may even react correctly. But the Communists demand far more than correct and docile obedience. The fact that Communist cadres are constantly urged to fight against "apathy" or "indifference" among the masses suggests that a kind of passivity exists which the regime does not and cannot tolerate.

Mass persuasion in Communist China is far from a complete success, and the system of communication is far less effective than its inventors had expected. A casual review of the Chinese Communist press discloses ample evidence of serious problems and difficulties that have profoundly disturbed the rulers in Peking. There are, for instance, frequent and open complaints that many Party comrades still "cannot grasp the usefulness of the work of persuasion"; that too many of them are unimaginative, superficial, impatient, or downright sloppy with their political and ideological tasks; that much of their persuasion work is "outwardly impressive but basically ineffective"; that there is too much formalism and routine in propaganda; and that too many of the Party cadres are still themselves "victims of erroneous ideologies and harmful ideas." In the "Hundred Flowers" campaign in 1957–58, there were enough complaints to fill several volumes.

There is some element of truth in the following testimony of a businessman educated in America, who, on going to China, was first enthusiastic about and then disgusted with Communism, who somehow managed to outwit the Communists' indoctrination, and who finally fled Red China:

Anyone who believes that "brainwashing" or "thought reform" were used successfully to make 650 million Chinese *believe* in Communism needs only to read the Chinese newspapers for May, 1957. The authorities obviously had been frightened by the fact that in Hungary, the people had risen against a "people's regime." This indicated that despite the continual use of brute force to suppress the masses, a Communist regime was not secure from a mass uprising. To forestall such uprising in China, the authorities acted upon the idea that permitting the people a kind of emotional catharsis would release harmlessly any latent impulse to violence. They also apparently believed that after eight years of enforced subservience the people must be docile enough so as not to dare to voice criticism of the regime in any extreme fashion. What the authorities did not realize was that even a slight release of pressure was almost sure to have an explosive effect. Within two weeks, therefore, the "speaking out" developed into a hysterical scream of protest.[1]

Bits and pieces of evidence in the Communist press suggest that the Peking regime is genuinely concerned with the "formalism" and routine of their mass persuasion. For in both regular political studies and in special indoctrination campaigns, the propagandists seem merely to go through the necessary motions, while the people dutifully and ritualistically react. After all the proper things have been said and done, after the stated objectives seem to be accomplished, both the propagandists and the people automatically and habitually move on to another cycle of the never-ending game.

But even the successful elimination of routine and other admitted difficulties will not necessarily mean that the Communist regime will have attained a perfect system for reshaping the thoughts and actions of the Chinese people. The truth of the matter is that while persuasive and coercive communications are powerful tools of indoctrination and control, they have definite limits.

One inherent limitation is that no matter how shrewdly propaganda is designed and how vigorously it is utilized, it "does not change conditions, but only beliefs about conditions, and it cannot force the people to change their beliefs but can only persuade them to do so."[2] One must therefore ask: Are the actual conditions in Communist China today as good as they are claimed to be? As one leading specialist on Chinese Communism points out:

> A major source of trouble besetting the Communists is their double-talk. They talk democracy but practice dictatorship; they stress voluntarism and exercise compulsion; and they preach freedom while they apply rigid control. Theirs is the double-talk of democratic dictatorship, the people's democratic state, and freedom of speech in a people's democracy. This Communist double-talk inevitably increases the inner contradictions of their regime. It is in the nature of the Communist ideology to try to ride horses racing in two opposite directions, the horse of "democracy" and the horse of "democratic dictatorship." This may well unsaddle them.[3]

Ironically, perhaps, the Chinese Communists may be trapped by their own successful persuasion. By their incessant use of persuasive communications, the Communists have stirred up much of the old, traditional China; they have turned millions of unconcerned, conciliatory, and easy-going peasants and workers into aggressive, agitated, and vicious fighters and revolutionaries; they have introduced a type of political activity and a pattern of socialization that had never existed in the country. The slumber of a sleeping China, to use an outworn cliché, is rudely disturbed. But once awakened, the nation cannot be expected to return immediately to its old inertia. Once a man becomes a converted revolutionary or trained rebel, he is not likely to be submissive again and unresisting. It may be that the tremendous power unleashed by the Chinese Communists and the new forces they have set in motion will eventually prove too much to handle. It is an old Chinese proverb that those who teach boxing are often floored by their pupils. The Chinese Communists have taught the people a great deal about the art of revolution.

Winds always shift direction, and a political wind cannot be expected to blow forever in one direction. When it does shift, it is not likely that the new direction will remain constantly favorable to those who rule. This metaphor reminds us of the observations made first by Merle Fainsod and, now more specifically, by Alex Inkeles, on political and public opinion in Soviet Russia:

> The figure most apt for describing the state of Soviet public opinion is that of a forest fire. On the broad peripheral front the blaze rages in full intensity. Here is found a thin line of convinced and confirmed Communists. But behind this line comes a much larger area, which has already been swept by the flames and which now boasts only glowing embers. This is the line of the half-believers, which includes some party members as well as the non-party supporters of the regime. And beyond that there lies a still broader sweep of the burned-over timber, in which here and there a spark still glows but which is prdominantly cold, ashen, and gray. The work of mass persuasion is the wind which fans this blaze. But like the wind in the forest fire, it not only spreads the flames but hastens the burning, and behind the line of flames and embers it can only stir up little swirls and eddies of ash.[4]

Essentially the same thing can be said about the situation in China.

It is hazardous to speculate on the future of mass persuasion in Communist China. But even if everything else should remain unchanged—which is unlikely—it will be, after another decade or two, vastly different. A new generation with no obvious or strong emotional ties to the past will have grown to adulthood. They will have learned from early childhood to follow the Party without questioning. Their thinking will not have to be "remolded." And by that time, the regime will have also gained more experience in improving their control and in using their system of persuasive and coercive communications. It is a chilling thought.

But one may seek some comfort in the fact that after decades of persuasion and rigid isolation, the propagandists in Moscow have yet to capture the minds and hearts of the young in the Soviet Union. The mind of man has a strange way of resisting oppression, and it is not likely that this characteristic will cease to exist altogether. But this is a problem that is infinitely larger than Communism itself.

APPENDIX

In order to assess the importance of *Jen Min Jih Pao*, one needs some understanding of its functions as defined by the Communists themselves. The following story about the newspaper appeared in the official *People's China*,* an English-language biweekly published in Peking for readers abroad. After wading through the jungle of Communist double-talk, one can get some insight into the planning behind China's most powerful newspaper, as well as a taste of Peking's peculiar brand of journalism. The story is a marvelous example of the Communists' own admission of how this propaganda instrument helps them to run the country:

THE PEOPLE'S DAILY

Every day at daybreak, a stream of post-office vans, motorcycles and bicycles loads up with copies of the *People's Daily* outside the office of the paper on Chang An Street, one of Peking's main thoroughfares. Then they speed to the railway station, the airport, and local distribution points to get the daily to its readers—members of the Communist Party, Youth League members, workers, peasants, intellectuals and cadres of government offices and people's organizations all over the country.

The *People's Daily* is the official organ of the Central Committee of the Communist Party of China. It was called the *Guide* in the period of the First Revolutionary Civil War (1924–27); the *Struggle* in the period of the Second Revolutionary Civil War (1927–36); the *New China Daily* in the period of the War of Resistance to Japanese Aggression (1936–45) and the *Liberation Daily* during the Liberation War. The *People's Daily* in its present

* January 16, 1954, pp. 12–16.

form was founded in 1948, when the people's revolutionary forces were approaching their final victory in the War of Liberation. Throughout its history, this organ of the Central Committee of the Chinese Communist Party has been closely linked with the revolutionary struggle of the Chinese people, showing the laboring people where the truth lies and illuminating the path to victory.

Since the victory of the people's revolution, the material and technical basis and the working conditions of the editorial department of the paper have been fundamentally improved. In Yenan, the *Liberation Daily* had its editorial department in a cave. Its whole staff numbered no more than fourteen persons. Using a handpress, they published only 8,000 copies a day. Today, in its fine new headquarters, the *People's Daily* has a staff of 270 in its editorial department, and a printing works with a staff of 400 persons. Its rotary press prints its daily edition of 550,000 copies in two and a half hours.

The *People's Daily* gives an authoritative picture of the political, economic and cultural life of the broad masses of the Chinese People. It publishes and explains the decisions made by the Communist Party of China and the Central People's Government in leading the Chinese people in their gradual transition to a Socialist society; it also explains in broad terms theoretical and practical problems concerning the Party and national construction. It keeps its readers informed about the achievements made by the Soviet Union and the People's Democracies in their peaceful construction, the struggle of the people in the colonial and semi-colonial countries for national liberation and the struggle for the defence of peace waged by the people throughout the world. The paper has played an immense role in educating the cadres and the broad masses of the laboring people.

Aids Marxist Education

Great attention is paid in the columns of the *People's Daily* to the propagation of the theory of Marxism-Leninism and the teachings of Mao Tse-tung. It has, for instance, printed the full texts of Stalin's works *Marxism and Linguistics* and *Economic Problems of Socialism in the U.S.S.R.* as well as a great deal of supplementary material. It has printed the full texts of Mao Tse-tung's works,

On People's Democratic Dictatorship, On Contradiction, On Practice, and others. It regularly publishes special articles on the theory of Marxism-Leninism, on problems of philosophy, history, literature and art, etc. One of its main tasks is to combat all ideological misrepresentations or distortions of Marxism-Leninism. In 1951, a film, *The Life of Wu Hsun,* which had serious defects of outlook, was produced. It sang the praises of Wu Hsun, a man who, in effect, served the interests of the feudal reactionary forces at the close of the nineteenth century. Wu Hsun, in the guise of a friend of the people, actually opposed the peasants in their armed struggle, and tried to inveigle them into a compromise with the ruling classes. When it was publicly released, this film was acclaimed by people under the influence of bourgeois ideology. The *People's Daily,* however, severely criticized this film in its editorial columns. At the same time, it sponsored a discussion to clarify the true nature of Wu Hsun's historic role. Cultural workers in all parts of the country participated in this discussion, which lasted for four months. In that time, more than a thousand articles and letters bearing on the subject were sent to the paper. This discussion played an important role in raising the ideological level of the intellectuals and the broad masses of the Chinese people.

Criticism and Self-Criticism

One of the special columns of the *People's Daily* runs under the general heading of "Party Life." This carries articles passing on experience in Party work in various enterprises and government offices, and describing the activities of outstanding Party members. It has printed stories about people like Chao Kuei-lan, who risked her life to save her factory from an explosion; model Communist member Wu Yun-to, China's "Pavel Korchagin"; Divisional Commander Cheng Yueh-chang, hero of the People's Liberation Army; and Yen Ming, a Communist of peasant origin, who, on account of his excellent work, was promoted by the Party to a leading post in a big factory. The column also levels sharp criticism against backward Party organizations and Party members who have fallen short of their duty, showing them how to correct their errors and overcome defects in their work. Severe criticism was directed, for example, against the errors of Li Sze-hsi, a Party member and village cadre in Hunan Province, who, after the victory of land reform, fell victim to the idea that the revolution "was over," and lost enthusiasm for revolutionary work. A penetrating analysis of this backward outlook of Li Sze-hsi was printed in the column, and this, according to many comments and letters received by the editorial board from Party members of peasant origin all over the country, helped many to see what lies in the further perspective of the revolution—the bright future of Socialism.

Consistently carrying out the "Decision Concerning the Promotion of Criticism and Self-criticism in the Press" promulgated by the Central Committee of the Communist Party in 1950, the *People's Daily* runs another special column entitled "Letters to the Editor." This prints letters from readers in various places criticizing defects in Party or government organizations. The column also carries the replies of the organizations concerned to the criticisms made. Letters of this kind are extremely helpful in revealing and eradicating defects in the work of various enterprises, government organizations and institutions. For instance, as a result of a letter from two readers in Shanghai that was printed by the *People's Daily,* a machine which was lying idle in a textile machinery factory was transferred to an iron and steel plant which happened to need just such a machine. Another letter from a reader in Tientsin exposed the fact that a wagon-load of cotton prints was destroyed by fire caused by negligence of workers in a certain state-owned company. As a result of the criticism raised by the *People's Daily,* the company made a thorough investigation into the case and worked out measures to eliminate defects in its work. When the *People's Daily* carried a letter from peasant readers in Shantung reporting cases of poisoning caused by the insecticide used in the villages, the local people's government promptly took countermeasures to deal with this danger.

The *People's Daily* also wages an effective campaign against those who try to stifle criticism. In the spring of 1953, a student of the Institute of Communications in Shanghai wrote to the *People's Daily* criticizing administrative work in the school. When the letter was published, the president of the school, who was concurrently Director of the Department of Communications of the former East China Military and Administrative Committee, took vindictive measures toward this student. When the Party took up the matter, he adopted a hostile and uncooperative attitude. The *People's Daily*, after an investigation, found out the true facts and consistently supported the criticism made by the student. Eventually the arrogant president was expelled from the Party and was also dismissed from his post by the administrative authorities. In an editorial entitled *Those Who Suppress Criticism Are the Party's Sworn Enemy*, the *People's Daily* called upon all Party members to develop criticism and self-criticism extensively and to wage a resolute struggle against all attempts to suppress criticism as this is detrimental to the interests of the party.

In the Struggle for Peace

The *People's Daily* mobilizes the people in the struggle for world peace. Since 1950, when the Chinese people launched the great movement to resist U.S. aggression and aid Korea, the work of mobilizing the people to support this lofty struggle has become an important task of the paper.

In addition to day-to-day reporting, the *People's Daily* issues a weekly supplement called "Resist U.S. Aggression and Aid Korea." This one-page feature carries stories of the heroic struggle of the Korean people and their Army and the Chinese People's Volunteers against the aggressors; reports of the warm support of peace-loving peoples of the world for the Korean people and other related items.

By this consistent coverage of one of the great mass movements of the day, the *People's Daily* helps its readers to understand that, only by winning the struggle to resist U.S. aggression and aid Korea, can they safeguard the peaceful construction of China and peace in the Far East and throughout the world. The paper has played a most important role in organizing and inspiring the masses for this great struggle.

Popularizing the General Line

In 1953, China completed the rehabilitation of its national economy and began its first five-year plan of national economic construction. The Communist Party and the Central People's Government of China drew up in more definite terms a general line of policy for the development of the country during its transition to

Socialism. The general line provides for the gradual realization of the Socialist industrialization of the country and the carrying out of Socialist transformation by the state of agriculture, handicraft production, and private industry and commerce step by step over a relatively long period. The *People's Daily* has paid great attention to the popularization of this general line. It explains the objective of the general line and the road that must be followed in bringing about the gradual Socialist industrialization of the country and the Socialist transformation of agriculture, handicraft production, and private industry and commerce. It has brought to its readers' attention the experience in Socialist construction of the Soviet Union and the People's Democracies.

This coverage is supplemented by daily reports on concrete achievements in national economic construction and by popularizing advanced experience in production. There are reports on the Anshan Iron and Steel Company's works, that great centre of China's new heavy industry, and systematic coverage of other newly rising industrial enterprises. Every issue carries articles describing the work of outstanding men and women workers and engineers. Recent reportage has introduced such nationally famous model workers as Ma Heng-chang, leader of a work brigade in a machine-building factory, which has consistently overfulfilled its quotas; the coal miner Ma Liu-hai, who set a new record for speed in tunnelling; the girl spinner Ho Chien-hsiu, who invented a new working method; and engineer Lan Tien, to whom a great share of the credit must go for mapping out the route of the Chengtu-Chungking Railway.

Help to Peasants

The *People's Daily* gives great help to the peasants. It makes known to them the policies of the Party and the People's Government in the development of China's rural areas. It tells them why and how they should follow the road to the future pointed out by Chairman Mao Tse-tung in his work *Getting Organized*. It also reports on the achievements of outstanding members of mutual-aid teams, agricultural producers' cooperatives and collective farms. At the same time, it levels its criticism against those rural cadres who deviate from the Party line, and, because of their wrong outlook and working style, use methods of compulsion and of giving bad commands in organizing and guiding the peasants. On February 15, 1953, the paper carried the *Decisions on Mutual Aid and Cooperation in Agricultural Production Adopted by the Central Committee of the Communist Party of China* and an editorial entitled *Key to Guidance of Agricultural Production.* This document and the editorial were of exceptional importance and they have become the key guide for rural Party organizations in their work of organizing and guiding the peasants.

A great deal of space is given in the *People's Daily* to the popularization of the advanced experience of the best peasant farmers. Recent coverage includes the new irrigation methods of peasant Tien Cheng-hsian of Shansi Province; the methods of champion cotton-grower Chu Yao-li and of the Shan-tung peasants who have gained big increases in wheat yield by applying the close-planting method of the Soviet Union; the successful methods of exterminating locusts used in Anhwei Province, and the good results achieved in forest protection in Northeast China.

Another important topic which finds space in the *People's Daily* is the policy on nationalities adopted by the Chinese Communist Party and the Central People's Government. Regular roundups are given on the achievements of the national minorities in building a free and happy life since their liberation from the yoke of the Kuomintang reactionaries.

The *People's Daily* also gives consistent attention to reporting on the cultural and educational achievements of the Chinese people and the development of their science, art and literature. Coverage is given to the activities of the universities, secondary and primary schools; achievements of the Soviet Union and the People's Democracies in their development of science, culture and art, and the application of Soviet educational methods in the schools of China.

Close Contacts With Readers

Opinions of representative people of all strata of society are fully reflected in the columns of the *People's Daily*. It has a broad range of active contributors from among the workers, peasants, scholars, writers, cadres, fighters of the People's Liberation Army and of the Chinese People's Volunteers, model workers, students and many others. Regular contact is maintained by its editorial department with more than ten thousand correspondents scattered throughout the country. Over 200,000 contributions received by the editorial department in the past four years came from workers and peasants. This is in addition to more than four hundred letters received from readers every day and the average of twenty readers who call every day at the office. The *People's Daily* prides itself on taking prompt and appropriate action on all matters raised in readers' letters and by its many visitors, so that defects and mistakes pointed out by its readers may be quickly rectified.

The most varied matters are brought up in letters and by visitors. An agricultural mutual-aid team reports on its rich harvest; a worker criticizes the bureaucratic style of work of the factory management. A group of fighters of the People's Liberation Army protests against the bacteriological warfare waged by the U.S. aggressors. Students of a whole class express their determination to devote themselves on graduation to construction in the border regions of the motherland. . . .

Readers Abroad

The *People's Daily* keeps regular contact with its readers abroad and its subscribers scattered in more than twenty foreign countries. It constantly carries articles on important international issues, and it gives the views of the Chinese people on current international affairs. It makes known the foreign policy of the People's Government of China, which is directed against all wars of aggression and stands for the settlement of international disputes through negotiation and the maintenance of peace among all peoples.

For the past four years, the *People's Daily* has devoted a great deal of attention to introducing its readers to China's great ally, the Soviet Union. How vast is the interest of the people in this coverage is shown by the thousands of letters which have been received from readers expressing their common belief that: "The Soviet Union's today is our tomorrow."

The *People's Daily* reflects the gratitude of the Chinese people for the sincere and selfless help given them by the Soviet Union.

It systematically publishes letters from its readers addressed to their Soviet friends. Following Chairman Mao Tse-tung's instructions on "learning from the Soviet Union," the *People's Daily* has devoted many of its columns to introducing the advanced experience of the Soviet Union to its readers. It has carried many important editorials of the *Pravda* in the past four years, and runs a special column for articles and commentaries reprinted from the Soviet press.

Special space is devoted to the achievements of peaceful construction in the Soviet Union and the People's Democracies.

Readers can also be sure of getting reports on the labour movement in capitalist countries, on the struggle for liberation of the people in colonial and dependent countries, and the great struggle for peace waged by all peoples.

Holding high the banner of Marxism-Leninism, the *People's Daily* inspires its millions of readers in their struggle for the bright tomorrow. It rallies the labouring masses around the Communist Party that is leading the Chinese people in the advance to the Socialist future.

NOTES

Chapter I: The Role and Nature of Mass Persuasion

1. Friedrich and Brzezinski refer to this as "passion for unanimity," which, they observe, "makes the totalitarians insist on the complete agreement of the entire population under their control to the measures the regime is launching." They add that "the totalitarian regimes insist that enthusiastic unanimity characterize the political behavior of the captive populations." See Carl J. Friedrich and Zbigniew K. Brzezinski, *Totalitarian Dictatorship and Autocracy* (Cambridge: Harvard University Press, 1956), p. 132.

2. *Jen Min Jih Pao* (*People's Daily*, Peking), editorial, November 11, 1960.

3. *Ibid.*, May 26, 1958.

4. *Ibid.*, April 28, 1958. This refers to the *chiao hsin yun tung* (Campaign to Give Hearts), supposedly initiated by the "democratic parties" in China following the "Hundred Flowers" campaign in 1958, as a pledge of their loyalty to the Party.

5. *Ibid.*, August 10, 1957. This is a story about the problem of food distribution in the rural areas of Hunan. The Chinese headline reads: *chieh-chueh ssu-hsiang wen-ti, chu lun chieh-chueh liang-shih wen-ti.*

6. *Ibid.*, September 13, 1960. This is a direct translation of the Chinese version which reads: *cheng chih kwa shuai, kang tieh tseng chan.* It is about the campaign to increase the production of iron and steel in Shanghai.

7. *Ibid.*, January 24, 1961.

8. Mao Tse-tung, *On People's Democratic Dictatorship* (Peking: English Language Service, New China News Agency, 1949), p. 13.

9. "The Basic Working Method of the Party," *Jen Min Jih Pao*, March 5, 1951.

10. Yu Kuang Yuan, "To Develop the Ideological Education of Marxism-Leninism from the Discussions on the Story of Wu Hsuen," *Hsueh Hsi* (*Study*, Peking), IV, Nos. 6–7 (June 1, 1951), 59.

11. *Peking Review*, No. 14, June 3, 1958.

12. Ma T'ieh-ting, *Ssu Hsiang Tsa T'an* (*Miscellaneous Talks on Ideology*) (Hankow: Wuhan Popular Books Publishing Co., 1951), Book V, 11–13.

13. Robert K. Merton, Marjorie Risk, and Alberta Curtis, *Mass Persuasion: The Social Psychology of a War Bond Drive* (New York: Harper, 1946); also, Dorwin Cartwright, "Some Principles of Mass Persuasion," *Human Relations*, 1949, No. 2, 253–67; also available in Daniel Katz *et al.*,

eds., *Public Opinion and Propaganda* (New York: The Dryden Press, 1954), pp. 382–93.

14. Walter Lippmann, *The Public Philosophy* (Boston: Little, Brown, 1955).

15. C. Wright Mills, *The Power Elite* (New York: Oxford University Press, 1956).

16. Carl I. Hovland, Irving L. Janis, and Harold H. Kelley, *Communication and Persuasion* (New Haven: Yale University Press, 1953); also, C. I. Hovland *et al.*, *The Order of Presentation in Persuasion* (New Haven: Yale University Press, 1957).

17. The most recent and thorough study on this problem is Theodore H. E. Chen, *Thought Reform of the Chinese Intellectuals* (Hong Kong University Press, 1960). Other interesting and significant studies are:

"Brainwashing," *Journal of Social Issues* (special issue), XIII, No. 3 (1957), articles by Robert J. Lifton, Edgar H. Schein, Julius Segal, Raymond A. Bauer, and James G. Miller; L. E. Hinkle and H. G. Wolff, "Communist Interrogation and Indoctrination of the 'Enemies of the State,'" *Archives of Neurology and Psychiatry*, LXXVI (1956), 115–74.

Joost A. M. Merloo, "Brainwashing in Perspective: A Psychiatrist Interprets Peking's 'Thought Reform,'" *The New Republic*, No. 136 (May 13, 1957), 21–25; "Thought Reform of Western Civilians in Chinese Communist Prisons," *Psychiatry*, XIX (1956), 173–96, and; "Home by Ship: Reaction Patterns of American Prisoners of War Repatriated from North Korea," *American Journal of Psychiatry*, CX (1954), 732–39.

Edgar H. Schein (with Inge Schneier and Curtis H. Barker), *Coercive Persuasion* (New York: W. W. Norton, 1961); "The Chinese Indoctrination Program for Prisoners of War," *Psychiatry*, XIX (1956), 149–72; "Interpersonal Communication, Group Solidarity and Social Influence," address delivered to the International Council for Women Psychologists, August 28, 1958, Washington, D. C. (mimeographed), and; M. T. Singer and E. H. Schein, "Projective Test Responses of Prisoners of War Following Repatriation," *Psychiatry*, XXI (1958), 375–85.

H. A. Segal, "Initial Psychiatric Findings of Recently Repatriated Prisoners of War," *American Journal of Psychiatry*, CXI (1954), 358–63.

I. E. Farber, H. F. Harlow, and L. J. West, "Brainwashing, Conditioning and DDD (Debility, Dependency, and Dread)," *Sociometry*, XX (1957), 271–85; Edouard Sanvage, *Dans les Prisons Chinoises* (1957).

18. Walt Rostow observes:

Having seized the instruments of power, isolating potentially hostile elements and rendering them ineffective, the Communists simultaneously began to build what they believed were the popular foundations for their rule. There appears to be an element of distinct ideological faith reflected in this first phase of Chinese Communist policy. The leaders appeared to believe that a shift in social power among Chinese classes, combined with an intense and monopolistic flow of propaganda and re-education, would bring about a situation where, in some sense, the Communists might rule by consent. By 1949 Moscow had long since abandoned any serious effort to induce desired popular actions within the Soviet Union by propaganda devices which would make men act out of enthusiasm and by direct personal identification with the motives and purposes of the Communist state.

Such efforts had been superseded by appeals to material advance, power, prestige, and nationalism, and by the threatening consequences of failure to conform. The Chinese Communists, at least briefly, sought to generate a mood of positive acceptance and enthusiasm, possibly as a cynical tactic to cover the period until full-scale machinery of control and coercion was installed, but possibly also in the hope that a measure of real persuasion could be achieved.
The Prospects for Communist China (Cambridge and New York: Technology Press of Massachusetts Institute of Technology and John Wiley & Sons, Inc., 1954), p. 63.

19. Edgar Faure, *The Serpent and the Tortoise* (New York: St. Martin's Press, 1958), p. 76.

Chapter 2: Theory and Policy

1. Wilbur Schramm, *Responsibility in Mass Communication* (New York: Harper and Brothers, 1957), p. 81.

2. Ai Ssu-ch'i, *Li Shih Wei Wu Lun She Hui Fa Chan Shih Chiang I* (*Historical Materialism: Lectures on History of Social Development*) (1st rev. ed.; Peking: Workmen's Publishing Co., June, 1951), pp. 83–86.

3. Oscar Glantz, "Class Consciousness and Political Solidarity," *American Sociological Review*, XXIII, No. 4 (August, 1958), 375–83.

4. "Unless class consciousness is present then no matter what criterion we take, we have not a social class but a mere logical category or type." R. M. MacIver, *Society* (New York: Farrar and Rinehart, 1937), p. 167.

5. See Emile Durkheim, *The Rules of Sociological Method*, trans. S. A. Solovay and J. H. Mueller (Chicago: University of Chicago Press, 1938).

6. Glantz, *op. cit.*, p. 376.

7. See Jean-Marie Domenach, "Leninist Propaganda," *Public Opinion Quarterly*, Summer, 1951.

Inkeles also makes this point very clearly:

The Marxist orientation assumes that the most important aspect of human society is its "material base," the relationship of human beings to the productive forces. One should not neglect the fact, however, that the Marxist approach assumed that material influences were always mediated through consciousness. This, in one sense, constitutes what you may call an idealist element within the Marxist materialist philosophy. . . .

If we turn to the Leninist variant on this orientation, we see a movement which is in a certain sense consistent and has important implications for a propaganda policy. Leninism to a large extent replaced the determinism of Marx with heavy emphasis on voluntarism. The Leninist position essentially held that one could not sit around and wait for the revolution to come spontaneously, but rather one must go out and organize it. The Leninist changed the orientation toward consciousness of the Marxist theory to emphasize that consciousness was not automatically developed in the proletariat. Rather, consciousness had to be brought from without to the proletariat, brought to it by a special and select elite group, namely, the trained Marxist. In other words, there was to be some carrier or agent of consciousness. Finally, he emphasized that there had to be some organization which would be essential to bringing consciousness to the masses, in some sense as acting as midwife at the revolutionary birth of the new society. That organization was, of course, the Communist Party. Alex Inkeles, "Communist Propaganda and Counter Propaganda," *Proceedings of the 28th Institute of the Norman Wait Harris Memorial Foundation* (1952), stenographic transcript (on file, Social Relations Reading Room, Harvard University).

8. Liu Shao-chi, *On the Party* (Peking: Foreign Languages Press, 1950), pp. 57–58.

9. Ai Ssu-ch'i, *op. cit.*, p. 126.

10. Wu Ching-chao, Yang Jen-ken, Lai Hai-tsung and others, eds., *T'u Ti Kai Ke Yu Ssu Hsiang Kai Tsao (Land Reform and Thought Reform)* (Peking: Kuang Ming Jih Pao She, 1951), p. 30.

11. Liu Shao-chi, "Report on the Problem of Land Reform," *T'u Ti Kai Ke Ch'ung Yao Wen Hsien Hui Chi (Collection of Important Documents of Land Reform)* (Peking: Jen Min Ch'u Pan She, 1951), pp. 11–28.

12. A statement released by the South China Sub-Bureau of the Chinese Communist Party. The complete title is "The Proposal Concerning the Strengthening of the Ideological Mobilization Tasks Among Peasants in Land Reform," *Nan Fang Jih Pao (Southern Daily,* Canton), December 26, 1951.

13. *Jen Min Jih Pao,* December 11, 1958.

14. *Selected Works of Mao Tse-tung* (London: Lawrence & Wishart, 1954), IV, 153.*

15. *Loc. cit.*

16. *Ibid.,* p. 113. This quotation is from a resolution on methods of leadership drafted by Mao on behalf of the Central Committee of the Communist Party. The resolution was passed on July 1, 1943, by the Party's Politburo. The Chinese text is available in the *Cheng Feng Wen Hsien (Documents of the Party's Ideological Remolding Movement)* (Hong Kong: Hsin Min Chu Ch'u Pan She, 1949), pp. 139–44.

17. *Chung Kuo Kung Chan Tang Chang Cheng (Constitution of the Chinese Communist Party)* (Peking: Jen Min Ch'u Pan She, 1956), p. 8.

18. Liu Shao-chi, *On the Party,* p. 44.

19. *Jen Min Jih Pao,* December 11, 1958.

20. Liu Shao-chi, *On the Party,* pp. 44–67.

21. *Ibid.,* pp. 63–64.

22. *Ibid.,* pp. 65–66.

23. Hu Sheng, Yu Kuang-yuan and Wang Hui-teh, "Strategy and Tactics of the Communist Party," Series No. 27 of "Lectures on the Fundamental Knowledge of Social Science," in *Hsueh Hsi (Study),* No. 1, 1952 (February 10, 1952), p. 41.

24. *Selected Works of Mao Tse-tung,* II, 222. This statement was made on November 5, 1938, and included in an article entitled "The Question of Independence and Autonomy within the United Front."

25. *Ibid.,* p. 218.

26. Mao Tse-tung, *On People's Democratic Dictatorship and Speech at the*

* Both the Chinese and English editions of Mao's works have been utilized in the preparation of this book. In the Notes, when the title appears in English, it refers to the Lawrence & Wishart edition; when in Chinese, to the edition published in Peking.

Preparatory Meeting of the New PCC (Peking: English Language Service, New China News Agency, 1949), p. 26.

27. Mao Tse-tung, "Introducing 'The Communist,'" in Mao Tse-tung and Liu Shao-chi, *Lessons of the Chinese Revolution* (Bombay: People's Publishing House, undated), pp. 5–6.

28. Chen Ren-bing, "New China's Thought Reform Movement," *China Monthly Review* (Shanghai), CXXII, No. 2 (February, 1952), 125.

29. Sung Kun-wu, "Participating in Public Trials," *Jen Min Chiao Yu* (*People's Education*), 1958, No. 6 (May 16, 1958), p. 32.

30. *Selected Works of Mao Tse-tung*, III, p. 92. From the article entitled "The Chinese Revolution and the Chinese Communist Party."

31. *Ibid.*, p. 91.

32. *Ibid.*, pp. 89–90.

33. Mao Tse-tung, *On People's Democratic Dictatorship*, p. 17.

34. Mao Tse-tung, "Introducing 'The Communist,'" pp. 6–7.

35. These two principles are discussed in *Hsueh Hsi* (*Study*) and very frequently referred to in Communist literature. See *Hsueh Hsi*, No. 1, 1952 (February 10, 1952), p. 42.

36. *Ibid.*, p. 41.

37. *Jen Min Jih Pao*, May 13, 1957; also available in *Hsin Hua Pan Yueh Kan* (*Hsin Hua Fortnightly*, Peking), No. 7, 1957, p. 35.

38. *Jen Min Shu Tse* (*People's Yearbook*, 1951) (Shanghai: Ta Kung Pao, 1951), p. 11.

39. This movement was reported almost daily from February 13 to April 11, 1955, in *Jen Min Jih Pao*.

40. *Hsueh Hsi, loc. cit.*

41. *Mao Tse-tung Hsien Chi* (*Selected Works of Mao Tse-tung*), I, 276.

42. Professor Gablentz has made an interesting analysis of Communist ideology on the basis of the unusually revealing comment of Bishop Lilje when he said that Communism was "elementary, precise, and binding." Communism is elementary, "for it reduces its system to a few simple formulae"; precise, because "it claims to be a science and it is at least methodical"; and binding, because "from this knowledge [of history and society] follows the necessity for action . . . : the young Marx formulated the inflammatory thesis that it was now time to change the world, which the philosophers had hitherto merely interpreted." See Otto Gablentz (Director of the German Academy of Politics), "Why Is There no Western Ideology?" *Universitas* (A German Review of the Arts and Sciences, Quarterly English Languages Edition), II, No. 1 (1958), 31–36.

43. *Hsueh Hsi*, p. 44.

44. Shen Chun-ju, "To Guarantee the Enforcement of Our Marriage Law," Commission on Legal and Legislative Affairs of the Central People's Government, ed., *Hun Yin Fa Chi Ch'i Yu Kuan Wen Chien* (*Marriage Laws and Related Documents*) (Peking: Hsin Hua Shu Tien, 1960), p. 99.

45. *Chinese Literature* (Peking), No. 2, February, 1959.

46. See Mao Tse-tung, "On Contradiction," written in August, 1937, in *Mao Tse-tung Hsien Chi*, I, 287–326; and his "Regarding Correctly Solving the Problems of Internal Contradiction Among the People," written in 1957, in *Hsin Hua Pan Yueh Kan* (*Hsin Hua Fortnightly*), No. 13, 1957 (July 10, 1957), pp. 1–14.

47. *Chang Chiang Jih Pao* (*Yangtze Daily*, Hankow), July 14, 1951.

48. Fu Cheng-sheng, *Tung Pei Ch'u Chien Li Hsien Chuan Wang Ti Ching Yen* (*Experiences in Building up Propaganda Networks in the Northeast Region*) (Mukden: Tung Pei Jen Min Ch'u She, 1951), pp. 69–70.

49. Liu Shao-chi, *On the Party*, p. 5.

50. Daniel Lerner, "Effective Propaganda: Conditions and Evaluation," in Wilbur Schramm, *The Process and Effects of Mass Communication* (Urbana: University of Illinois Press, 1954), p. 480.

Chapter 3: The Background of Mass Persuasion

1. "Rectify the Party's Style in Work," *Selected Works of Mao Tse-tung*, IV, 44–45.

2. Mao, "Oppose the Party 'Eight-legged Essay,' " *ibid.*, p. 49.

3. Chu Min, *Ssu Hsiang Kai Tsou Hsueh Hsi* (*Thought Reform and Study*) (Shanghai: Ta Hua Publishing Co., 1952), p. 54.

4. Mao, "On Coalition Government," *ibid.*, pp. 313–14.

5. *Lun Tse Wo P'i P'ing* (*On Self-Criticism*) (October Publishing, 1950). (The location of the publisher is not given. The book is distributed by the Southern Bookstore in Kowloon, Hong Kong.)

6. For a list of the twelve volumes, see Theodore H. E. Chen, "Education and Propaganda in Communist China," *Annals of the American Academy of Political and Social Science*, CCLXXVII (September, 1951), p. 137.

7. See Lee Jui, *Mao Tse-tung Tung Chi Ti Tsu Chi K'e Min Ho Tung* (*Comrade Mao Tse-tung's Early Revolutionary Activities*) (Peking: Chin Nien Chu Pan She, 1957).

8. *Ibid.*, p. 103.

9. *Mao Tse-tung Hsien Chi*, I, 13–46.

10. *Ibid.*, pp. 36–37.

11. *Ibid.*, pp. 25–27.

12. "The Battle of Chingkanshan," *ibid.*, pp. 59–86.

13. *Ibid.*, p. 69.

14. *Ibid.*, p. 77.

15. *Ibid.*, p. 76.

16. "Regarding the Correction of Erroneous Ideas in the Party," *ibid.*, pp. 87–99.

17. *Ibid.*, p. 87.

18. "On Tactics of Fighting Japanese Imperialism," *ibid.*, p. 145.

19. "Strategical Problems of China's Revolutionary War," *ibid.*, p. 206.

20. "The Question of Independence and Autonomy within the United Front," *Selected Works of Mao Tse-tung*, II, 218–22.

21. *Ibid.*, pp. 220–21.

22. "The Tasks of the Chinese Communist Party in the Period of Resistance to Japan," *Mao Tse-tung Hsien Chi*, I, p. 254.

23. "Strive to Win Over Millions Upon Millions of the Masses to the Anti-Japanese National United Front," *ibid.*, p. 266.

24. *Loc. cit.*

25. *Ibid.*, p. 267.

26. According to Mao, the ideological struggle against Chang Kuo-tao's

line began at a meeting in August, 1935, at Pasi, northwest of the county town of Sungpan, situated between northwestern Szechuan and southeastern Kansu, and ended at an enlarged meeting of the Central Political Bureau of the Party held in Yenan in April, 1937. See "The Role of the Chinese Communist Party in the National War," *Selected Works of Mao Tse-tung*, II, 212.

27. *Ibid.*, p. 213.

28. *Ibid.*, p. 211.

29. Mao, "Strive to Win Over Millions Upon Millions of the Masses to the Anti-Japanese National United Front," *ibid.*, pp. 279–80.

30. "The Role of the Chinese Communist Party in the National War," *ibid.*, p. 208.

31. *Ibid.*, p. 215.

32. *Ibid.*, pp. 214–15.

33. Mao, "Introductory Remarks to *The Communist*," *Selected Works*, III, 53.

34. Mao, "An Introductory Remark to *The Chinese Worker*," *Selected Works*, III, 175–79.

35. "Introductory Remarks to *The Communist*," pp. 58–59.

36. Mao, *Selected Works*, IV, 12.

37. Lu Ting-i, "Fifteenth Anniversary of the Ideological Remoulding Movement," *Hsin Hua Pan Yueh Kan* (*New China Fortnightly*, Peking), No. 7, 1957, p. 52. The article was published originally in *Jen Min Jih Pao*, March 5, 1957.

38. "The Wild Lily" was published originally in *Chieh Fang Jih Pao* (*Liberation Daily*, Yenan), March 19 and 23, 1942. It is available in *Wen Yih Pao* (*Journal of Literature*, Peking), No. 2, 1958, pp. 5–7.

39. "Re-examination—An account of a protracted struggle in contemporary Chinese literature," *Chinese Literature* (Peking), May–June, 1958, No. 3, pp. 154–55.

40. *Ibid.*, pp. 156–57.

41. "Report of the Propaganda Department of the Central Committee of the Chinese Communist Party on the Cheng Feng Reform Movement," *Cheng Feng Wen Hsien* (*Party Reform Documents*) (China: Hsin Hua Bookstore, 1949), pp. 1–5.

42. "Re-examination—An account of a protracted struggle in contemporary Chinese literature," *op. cit.*, p. 158.

43. For a story of the Communist version of the Hsiao Chun case, see Liu Tse-ming, *Ching Suan Hsiao Chun Ti Fan Tung Ssu Hsiang* (*Liquidation of Hsiao Chun's Reactionary Ideology*) (Hong Kong: Sin Min Chu Publishing Co., 1949); Yen Wen-ching and Kung Mu, "Re-examination of Hsiao Chun's Ideology," *Wen Yi Pao* (*Literary Gazette*, Peking), No. 7, 1958, p. 36 (The appendix includes the three articles by Hsiao Chun that touched off the attack against him in 1948); and Ma Tieh-ting, "Regarding the article 'On Comradeship and Forebearance Among Comrades'—A Denunciation," *Wen Yi Pao*, No. 2, 1958, pp. 17–21.

44. *Wen Hua Pao* (*Culture News*, Harbin), No. 8, 1948.

45. "The Role of the Chinese Communist Party in the National War," *op. cit.*, p. 207.

46. "Questions of Tactics in the Present Anti-Japanese United Front," *Selected Works of Mao Tse-tung*, III, 194.

47. *Ibid.*, p. 196.
48. *Ibid.*, p. 198.
49. *Loc. cit.*
50. *Ibid.*, p. 202.
51. *Ibid.*, pp. 202–203.
52. *Ibid.*, p. 203.
53. "Freely Expand the Anti-Japanese Forces; Resist the Attacks of the Anti-Communist Die-hards," ibid., pp. 204–210.

Chapter 4: The Organizational and Operational Pattern

1. Mao Tse-tung, "Fan Tui Tang Pa Ku" ("Opposing Party Formalism") in *Cheng Fen Wen Hsien* (*Ideological Remolding Documents*) (Hong Kong: New Democracy Publishing Co., undated), p. 33.
2. Liu Shao-chi, *On the Party*, p. 136.
3. *Hsueh Hsi*, IV, No. 8 (August 1, 1951), p. 25.
4. *Hsin Hua Yueh Pao* (*New China Monthly*, Peking), III, No. 3 (January, 1951), pp. 507–509.
5. Editorial Department of the People's Publishing Co., ed., *Tsen Yang Tso Hsien Ch'uan Yuan* (*How to be a Propagandist*) (Peking: People's Publishing Co., 1951), pp. 11–12.
6. *Jen Min Jih Pao*, February 11, 1951.
7. *Ibid.*, December 21, 1951.
8. Editorial Department of the People's Publishing Co., *op. cit.*, p. 180.
9. Fu Cheng-sheng, *op. cit.*, pp. 13–14.
10. *Ibid.*, p. 19.
11. *Nan Fang Jih Pao* (*Southern Daily*, Canton), September 10, 1951.
12. Fu Cheng-sheng, *op. cit.*, p. 35.
13. *Jen Min Jih Pao*, August 20, 1951.
14. *Ibid.*, July 13, 1951.
15. *Ibid.*, editorial, December 19, 1951.

Chapter 5: Mass Communication: The System

1. Robert Guillain, *600 Million Chinese* (New York: Criterion Books, 1957), p. 137.
2. "Everything for the Convenience of Readers," *Jen Min Jih Pao*, editorial, March 16, 1958.
3. Yeh Chang-ching, "Land Reform and Language of Peasants," in Wu Ching-chao, Yang Jen-ken, Lai Hai-tsung and others, eds., *T'u Ti Kai Ke Yu Ssu Hsiang Kai Tsao* (*Land Reform and Thought Reform*), p. 109.
4. *Wen Hui Pao* (Shanghai), January 1, 1959.

Chapter 6: Mass Communication: The Press

1. George Stafford Gale, *No Flies in China* (New York: William Morrow & Company, 1955), pp. 136–37.
2. For a detailed discussion of the role of the press in the Soviet Union, see

Alex Inkeles, *Public Opinion in Soviet Russia* (Cambridge: Harvard University Press, 1950), pp. 135–222.

3. The letter was written on January 12, 1958, by Mao to two Party members in Honan. Wu Chi-pu, "Fully Develop the Five Functions of a Provincial Newspaper," *Hsin Hua Pan Yueh Kan* (*New China Fortnightly*, Peking), February 25, 1959, No. 4, p. 160.

4. Lu Ting-i, "Speech Delivered on the Twentieth Anniversary of the New China News Agency," *Jen Min Shu Tse* (*People's Handbook*) (Peking: Ta Kung Pao, 1958), p. 144.

5. Teng Kuo, "Socialist Revolution on the Journalistic Front," *Hsueh Hsi*, No. 8 (April 18, 1958), p. 2.

6. *Loc. cit.*

7. Li Yu-yin, ed., *Kao Teng Hsueh Hsiao Hsueh-sheng ti Hsueh Hsi Ho Sheng-wo* (*Study and Life of Students in Institutes of Higher Learning*) (Hong Kong: Sheng-wo, Tu-shu, Hsui Chih Publishers, 1955), p. 27.

8. *Ta Kung Pao* (Shanghai), April 24, 1950.

9. Alex Inkeles, *Public Opinion in Soviet Russia*, pp. 161–62.

10. Chin Tsao, *Tsen Yang Hsieh Hsin Wen Tung Hsun* (*How to Write Newspaper Correspondence*) (Changchaikuo: Hsin Hua Book Store, 1946), p. 4.

11. Liu Tseng-chi, "The Press in New China," *Culture and Education in New China* (Peking: Foreign Languages Press, undated), p. 43.

12. *Hsin Hua Yueh Pao* (*New China Monthly*, Peking), II, No. 4 (August, 1950), p. 901.

13. *Peking Wan Pao* (*Peking Evening News*), February 27, 1959.

14. "Directive from the Shanghai People's Municipal Government on Development of Self-Criticism in Newspapers," *Ta Kung Pao*, May 16, 1950.

15. Shen Yen-ping, "Achievements in Cultural and Art Work," speech delivered to the First Session of the Second National People's Congress on April 24, 1959. In American Consulate General (Hong Kong), *Current Background*, No. 577 (May 14, 1959).

16. American Consulate General, *Current Background*, No. 478 (October 28, 1957).

17. Franklin W. Houn, *To Change a Nation* (New York: Crowell-Collier, 1961), p. 123.

18. *Jen Min Jih Pao*, July 19, 1957.

19. "Fei Hsiao-tung and Chu An-ping Apologize to the People," *Jen Min Jih Pao*, July 14, 1957.

20. Lo Lung-chi, "My First Confession," *Jen Min Jih Pao*, July 16, 1957.

21. Chang Po-chun, "With My Head Low and Bowed, I Apologize to the People," *loc. cit.*

22. *Jen Min Jih Pao*, September 23, 1957.

23. *Ibid.*, January 4, 1958.

24. *Loc. cit.*

25. *Ta Kung Pao*, April 24, 1950.

26. *Loc. cit.*

27. New China News Agency, "Two Main Problems in News Agencies" (a letter to all branches and sub-branches), *Hsin Hua Yueh Pao*, II, No. 4 (August, 1950), p. 965.

28. Teng Kuo, "Socialistic Revolution on the Journalistic Front," *op. cit.*, p. 4.

29. Franklin W. Houn, *op. cit.*, p. 98. See also Wang Chia-hua, "New China News Agency on the March: An Article in Commemoration of the Agency's 20th Anniversary," *Survey of China Mainland Press*, No. 1,614 (September 20, 1957), pp. 3–7.

Chapter 7: Mass Communication: Radio

1. Sripati Chandra-sekhar, *Red China: An Asian View* (New York: Frederick A. Praeger, 1961), pp. 8–9.
2. According to a report made by Kuo Mo-jo before the Political Consultative Conference on June 17, 1950. *Ta Kung Pao*, June 21, 1950.
3. Mei Tso, "The Chinese People's Broadcasting System," *Culture and Education in New China*, p. 50.
4. *Radio Listener*, No. 7 (January, 1956), pp. 8–9.
5. For a detailed discussion on the radio-diffusion exchanges in Soviet Russia, read Alex Inkeles, *Public Opinion in Soviet Russia*, pp. 225–86. The same system is developed in other Communist countries. In Poland, for instance, "wired radio" is becoming increasingly important. See Robert C. Sorensen and Leszek L. Meyer, "Local Uses of Wired Radio in Communist-Ruled Poland," *Journalism Quarterly*, Summer, 1955, pp. 343–48.
6. Article 49 of the Common Program of the Chinese People's Consultative Conference.
7. Tso Yung, "Broadcasting in China," *People's China*, No. 22 (November 16, 1953), p. 29.
8. Mei Tso, *op. cit.*, pp. 49–53.
9. *Jen Min Jih Pao*, September 12, 1951.
10. *Chung Hua Jen Min Kung Ho Kuo Fa Tsan Kuo Min Chingchi Ti I K'e Wu Nien Chi Hua* (*The First Five Year Plan of Developing People's Economy of the Chinese People's Republic*) (Peking: Jen Min Publishing Co., 1955), p. 140.
11. *Ibid.*, p. 143.
12. New China News Agency Dispatch, December 24, 1956. Reported in the *Survey of China Mainland Press*, No. 1,204 (January 10, 1957), published by the American Consulate General in Hong Kong.
13. *Loc. cit.*
14. *Kuang Min Jih Pao* (*Kuang Min Daily News*, Peking), March 27, 1956. Translated and reported in the *Survey of China Mainland Press*, No. 1,271 (April 19, 1956).
15. *Loc. cit.*
16. *Loc. cit.*
17. *Loc. cit.*
18. Editorial, *Jen Min Jih Pao*, December 12, 1955.
19. *Jen Min Jih Pao*, January 4, 1956.
20. *Ibid.*, January 6, 1956.
21. *Kuang Min Jih Pao*, March 27, 1956.
22. *Jen Min Jih Pao*, January 4, 1956.
23. *Ibid.*, August 18, 1956.
24. *Ibid.*, January 4, 1956.
25. *Loc. cit.*
26. Frederick T. C. Yu, *A Brief Report on the Home Service Broadcasts of*

the Central People's Broadcasting Station in Peking, 1952 (mimeographed, on file at the University of Southern California), p. 35.

27. *Ibid.,* p. 8.
28. *Ibid.,* p. 9.
29. Wen Chi-tse, "People's Broadcasting During the Last Ten Years," *Hsin Hua Yueh Pao* (*New China Monthly*), October, 1955, p. 232.
30. Yu, *op. cit.,* pp. 24–30.
31. *Ibid.,* for a study of radio propaganda in Communist China in the early years.
32. *Kuang Po Chieh Mo Pao* (*Broadcasting Program,* Peking), No. 225 (August 8, 1959).

Chapter 8: Mass Communication: Tatzepao (*Posters*)

1. *Chinese Literature* (Peking), No. 6 (November–December, 1958), p. 14.
2. *Jen Min Jih Pao,* editorial, September 13, 1960.
3. *Hsueh Hsi,* No. 12 (June 18, 1958), p. 20.
4. *Ibid.,* p. 21.
5. The article first appeared in the Yugoslav newspaper *Slavenski Porocevalee,* August 19, 1958. The digest of this piece appeared in the *Shih Chieh Jih Pao* (*The World Daily,* San Francisco), March 18, 1959.
6. *Hsueh Hsi,* No. 12 (June 18, 1958), pp. 20–21.
7. *Jen Min Jih Pao,* November 23, 1957.
8. *Wen Hui Pao* (Shanghai), January 1, 1959.
9. *Jen Min Jih Pao,* March 28, 1958.
10. *Ibid.,* August 13, 1958.
11. *Ibid.,* September 25, 1957.
12. *Jen Min Wen Hsueh* (*People's Literature,* Peking), No. 103 (June, 1958), p. 37.
13. "Tatzepao in Schools," *Jen Min Chiao Yu* (*People's Education,* Peking), XCIII, No. 6 (May 16, 1958), p. 19.
14. *Jen Min Jih Pao,* March 28, 1958.
15. Ma La, "Party Secretary," *Mong Tsung* (*Wild Seeds*), December 5, 1957, p. 18.

Chapter 9: Mass Communication: Film

1. *Jen Min Jih Pao,* September 15, 1960. This is an important address delivered by Hsia Yen at the Second Session of the Congress of All-China Representatives of the Federation of Chinese Film Workers, on July 30, 1960. The full-page newspaper article reviews Communist China's film industry since the beginning of the Communist regime.
2. *Loc. cit.*
3. *Jen Min Jih Pao,* February 22, 1957.
4. *People's China* (Peking), No. 10 (May 16, 1955).
5. *Nan Fang Jih Pao* (*Southern Daily,* Canton), December 26, 1951.
6. *Ta Kung Pao* (Hong Kong), December 29, 1951.
7. *People's China,* February 16, 1954, p. 39.
8. The following Communist writings are particularly useful and interest-

ing: Yu Lin, "The Party's Leadership and Struggle in China's Film Industry before the Liberation," *Chung Kuo Tien Yin* (*Chinese Film*, Peking), No. 6, 1959, pp. 42–46; Hsia Yen, "History of Chinese Film and the Leadership of the Party," *Jen Min Jih Pao*, November 16, 1957.

9. Yao Hua, "New China's Films," *People's China*, III, No. 8 (April 16, 1951), p. 12.

Chapter 10: *Mass Communication: Art and Literature*

1. Mao Tse-tung, *Problems of Art and Literature* (New York: International Publishers, 1950), p. 33.

2. Lu Ting-i, "New China's Education and Culture," *Hsin Hua Yueh Pao*, II, No. 1 (May, 1950), pp. 159–62.

3. Mao Tse-tung, *Problems of Art and Literature*, pp. 18–38, *passim*.

4. Chou Yang, "Building a Socialist Literature," *Chinese Literature* (Peking), No. 4, 1956, p. 205.

5. Tien Han, "The Struggle on the Front of Dramatics Since the Establishment of the Nation 11 Years Ago and Future Tasks," *Jen Min Jih Pao*, September 9, 1960.

6. Chou Yang, "New Folk Songs Blaze a New Trail in Poetry," *Chinese Literature*, No. 6, 1958, p. 8.

7. *Ibid.*, p. 13.

8. *Ibid.*, pp. 9–10.

9. *Ibid.*, p. 11.

10. *Ibid.*, p. 13.

11. *Loc. cit.*

12. *Jen Min Jih Pao*, September 9, 1960.

13. *Loc. cit.*

14. "Art Fights for Korea," *People's China*, III, No. 1 (January 1, 1951).

15. *Jen Min Jih Pao*, July 21, 1958.

16. *Ibid.*, February 27, 1958.

17. *Ibid.*, September 13, 1958.

Chapter 11: *Conclusions*

1. Robert Loh (as told to Humphrey Evans), *Escape from Red China* (New York: Coward-McCann, 1962), pp. 296–97.

2. Daniel Lerner, "Effective Propaganda—Conditions and Evaluations," in Daniel Lerner, ed., *Propaganda in War and Crisis* (New York: George W. Stewart, 1951), p. 346.

3. Theodore H. E. Chen, *op. cit.*, p. 201.

4. Alex Inkeles, *Public Opinion in Soviet Russia*, p. 323.

INDEX

Accusation (and grievance) meetings, 18, 28, 32, 73, 84, 85, 100, 139

Agriculture; see Peasants, Land Reform

agricultural cooperatives, movement for, 27, 128

Ai Ssu-ch'i, 11, 13

All-China Federation of Artists and Writers, 63, 149

All-China Playwrights Association, 153

Anti-Japanese Political and Military Academy, 53

art and literature, 59, 67–68, 69, 148–53; and political indoctrination, 60, 148–51; propaganda paintings, 148; "revolutionary" and "bourgeois," 68; theater, 152–53; Yenan Literary Meeting, 149; see also Cultural Affairs, Culture for Propaganda, Ideological Remolding, Mass Organizations

artists and writers, 46, 55, 60–61, 67–68; and Kuomintang, 68–69; and propaganda-agitation, 60–61; serving with and as workers and peasants, 113, 149–50; see also Ideological Remolding

"attacking the landlords politically," 42

blackboard newspapers, 73, 76, 92, 94, 96, 125

Bourgeoisie, 20, 21–22, 48–49, 52–53; Petty-bourgeois Mentality, 12, 34, 44, 45, 47, 55–56, 59, 63; see also United Front

brainwashing, and prisoners of war, 7–8, 43

cadres, training of, 50–51

Central Party School at Yenan, 54

central tasks; see Unity of Theory and Practice

Chandra-sekhar, Sripati, 123

Chang Kuo-tao, 46–47; and "right opportunism," 50

Chang Po-chun, 118–19

Chang Tso-lin, 40

Chen Pai-cheng, 153

Chen Po-ta, 59

Chen Shao-yu (alias Wang Ming), 45, 59, 60

Chen Tu-hsiu, 39, 40, 41, 45

Chen Yun, 53, 58, 59

Cheng Feng; see Ideological Remolding

Chiang Kai-shek, 46, 47, 48, 66, 152

Chin Jen, 63

Ching Pang-hsien (alias Po Ku), 45, 59

Chou En-lai, 59

Chou Yang, 149, 150

Chu An-ping, 118–19

Chu Chiu-pai, 45

Chu Teh, 45, 46

Class consciousness, 11–15, 23, 28, 42, 43, 91, 139; elevating level of, 7, 11–14, 17, 18, 21, 27, 40, 48–49, 75, 107; and propaganda, 98; self-education in, 32, 100; see also Grievance meetings, Struggle, People's Communes

"correct thinking and correct action"; see Unity of Theory and Practice

183

DATE